# Recipes From Home

## Weight Loss with Grain Free and Blood Type Recipes

Ashley Carson and Yolanda Nash

# Table of Contents

# Introduction

Obesity and being overweight, even if not obese, is a major problem for so many people today. Part of the blame can go to the availability of junk food. Junk food is quick and easy to eat and cheap for the most part. People live such busy lifestyles and junk food provides sustenance to conquer hunger, albeit not in a healthy way. Busy lifestyles does not necessarily mean people are physically active. The majority of overweight people lead sedentary lives even if they are busy. Most sit behind desks all day. We find we face a health crisis when so many become overweight.

**Health Concerns of Being Overweight**

Excessive weight will take its toll on the body sooner or later. Health concerns, which may stem from being overweight, are high blood pressure, high blood sugar, high cholesterol, bone, muscle, and joint issues. These concerns can lead to other more damaging health issues such as cardiovascular disease, diabetes, arthritis, and more. Many of these health concerns can be treated or reversed by losing weight.

Weight loss programs come in many shapes and sizes. You have crash diets, and long term diets, and diets where you only eat a certain type of food, diets where you eat very little, and diets where you are so restricted failure is almost a sure thing. When a diet exists only for weight loss you can almost guarantee it will not work. Why? Because if you just diet long enough to lose the weight and then go back to your old eating habits, the weight will come back just as fast as you lost it.

**Lifestyle Changes**

A weight loss diet should not be called a weight loss diet. If you think of dieting in terms of doing it long enough to lose the weight you are not solving the problem. If you have a weight issue now it means that you must make a lifestyle change to correct it. Dieting is a good way to lose weight, but dieting is not a temporary fix. Dieting should be a permanent change. View your new diet as a lifestyle change. You need to determine to get on the diet and stay on the diet. This is the best way to lose the weight and maintain the weight loss.

**Why Grain Free and Blood Type Diet?**

Grain free dieting is a great way to lose weight. Grains are carbs and carbs turn to glucose in the blood, which ends up turning to fat. (Unless you exercise a lot and burn off the calories.) A grain free diet consists of most foods but avoids grains. People get their beneficial fiber through fresh fruits and vegetables instead. By avoiding grains weight loss is a given. A grain free diet is well balanced and satisfying. You never feel as if you are doing without.

The blood type diet plans receive a lot of controversy. Some believe the diets are not beneficial while others swear by it. The whole point of the blood type diet is to eat foods that agree with your particular blood type. The foods lists for the blood type diets consists of healthy nutritious foods such as fresh fruits, vegetables, lean meats, and even whole grains. By eating the foods for your blood type your body will behave better and you will be able to lose weight. Both diets are healthy and neither one include junk food.

Which diet should you try? Even though some of the blood type diet recipes include grains, some don't. You can mix and match and see which one makes you feel more satisfied. You have a good variety of recipes in this book enough to plan a menu at least a week or more in advance without repeating meals.

## Tips to Make the Diet a Success

Making dieting change is tough if you have a bad habit of eating the wrong foods. And eating the wrong foods is an addictive habit. Food addictions are just as powerful as addictions to smoking and or drinking alcohol. While you can stop suddenly and jump right into the diets, you may experience the unpleasant side effects of food addiction withdrawal. Sugar is one of the largest enemies to your diet. If you enjoy your sugar then you are addicted. If you eat a sugared food at least once a day, you have an addiction. This highly addictive food will not allow you to let go of it easily. Caffeine is another that is power with addiction. You can experience headaches and moodiness with withdrawals, not to mention the horrible intense cravings for it. These unpleasant withdrawal side effects cause so many to fail with their dieting changes. Instead of taking the chance with failure, you should work on weaning during the first weeks of your new diet.

To wean slowly means you will take about three weeks to stop eating the junk food and replace the junk food with nutritious food. A great way to do this is through slow elimination. Spend about five days eating the junk food only two times a day. Then spend the next five days eating it once a day. After that, spend a week eating the junk food once every other day. Then put two days between, then three and finally you will reach a point where you are only eating the junk food once a week. You may decide you no longer want the junk food before you reach that point and that's okay. The whole point is to avoid the unpleasant withdrawal side effects.

**Disclaimer**

You should always talk any diet changes over with your physician or health care provider. They can let you know if what you plan is good for you. All information in here is strictly just that, information. View it as information and seek counsel with your health care provider before making any health changes to your diet and lifestyle. As with any diet, it will only work if you get on it and stick with it.

# Section 1: Blood Type Diet

## How the Blood Type Affects Diet

The blood type diet has gained in popularity over the past two decades since Dr. Peter D'Adamo first came out with his book *4 Blood Types, 4 Diets, Eat Right 4 Your Type*. While the existence for the need for such a diet remains controversial, you will find strong advocates for it along with their blood type theories. However, at this point and time, there has been no actual scientific or medical research in depth to prove or disprove the theories that a person should stick with a particular diet based solely on their blood type. You can find plenty of support in the theory, just run an internet search about this and see all the websites that stand behind the theory that each blood type needs a certain type of diet.

Since we are discussing the blood type diet, it helps to know the different blood types. We will touch on different types for introduction purposes. First, the blood type is measured from the antigens, the proteins that exist on red blood cells. The blood types O, A, and B are the most common. When a person is blood type A only the type A antigens resides on the surface of the red blood cells. The same goes with type B. Type AB contains both. Blood type O contains neither. There is a third antigen called the Rh factor and it either exists or does not, thus you have the "positive" and "negative" ratings of blood types. Of all the blood types, "O positive" is the most common in the world, with A being a close second.

A naturopathic physician name Peter D' Adamo is the pioneer who first came up with the blood type diet theory, devising an entire diet system around a person's blood type. Many others follow along with the blood type diet theory that the need for a particular diet for each blood type has evolved through the years due to the changes in the environment and in people's methods of obtaining food. He proposes that if a person eats certain foods that go against their blood types they will become weak and the result can show up as diseases and even weight gain.

# What the Opposition Says About Blood Type Diets

Those who oppose the blood type diet theory claim they have sufficient evidence supporting their belief; however, again, there is no real scientific or medical research evidence to disprove the theory. Again, do a search for the opposition and find many who support the opposing claim as well. The opposition's main concern is the lack of nutrition balance in the type A and type O diets and the opposition feels that the blood type diets should not be followed for long periods. A newsletter put out by the Harvard Medical School recently cites the lack of scientific evidence for such diets. They question the theory asking what may happen if more than one blood type shows up in a family. This type of reasoning looks at two parents, where one may be (for an example) type O blood, and the other type A. No matter what blood type the child turns out to be, either A or O, it is believed they still have the predisposition of the same behavior as each parent's blood type.

Therefore, it is difficult to assume that a child with a parent with a different blood type as theirs would benefit from such a strict diet. They further reason that the diet may be beneficial if, and this is a big if, every single family member has the same blood type, and the blood type was handed down through the years from generation to generation. But this is rare, blood types vary as much as skin and hair color.

No diet is one hundred percent great without doing other things to live a healthy lifestyle. Diet is just a piece of the whole puzzle that makes up a complete person. Just choosing sensible foods is a start, meaning to choose fruits and vegetables, lean proteins and to stay away from processed and refined foods. Break bad habits such as smoking and drinking alcohol excessively. Sedentary lifestyles are unhealthy. People need to get up and move around in order to be healthy. Exercise is often overlooked and should be a part of every healthy regimen, even for those with limited physical mobility, being physically active is necessary. If there are physical limitations, seek the help of a physical therapist or a gym instructor to come up with an exercise routine just for you. Dieting, exercising, and healthy lifestyle choices all work together to make a person healthy and whole. Drinking plenty of water with any diet is a must too. Water helps to digest the foods and helps to clean the body. All these things work together, and in doing all of these things together you become healthier faster, reaching your health and fitness goals quicker.

Peter D'Adamo believes that if a person wishes to lose weight they need to eat foods that agree with their blood type, see his book Eat Right for Your Type. D'Adamo would be well served if he would run some actual scientific studies and clinical trials to prove his beliefs. Many people go on his diet and claim it helps, however to draw your own conclusions, you need to test it out for yourself. As with anything having to do with your health, always seek the advice of your healthcare provider before trying any new diet or exercise routine.

# Blood Types

As stated above type O is the most common. According to LivingStrong.com 46 % of the population is a type O. 39% is type A and only 11% is type B. Type AB is the rarest and less than 5% of the population has this type.

Type O blood was the original blood type for humanity as believed by Peter D'Adamo. He believes people with type O blood should eat diets rich in proteins and less in glutens. This is how our Stone Age ancestors ate. If you look at the Paleo Diet you will see many similarities to the blood type O diet plan. Type O people of old were hunters and big meat eaters. They did not garden much because they spent all of their time on the hunt. He further states that type A blood came along when people started farming the lands and growing more fruits and vegetables. Type A should focus on grains and vegetarian type foods. Type B is a variation between the two diets. Type AB should avoid legumes and certain grains and seeds. D'Adamo believes that by eating the wrong foods in conjunction with your blood type the result will be excessive body fat.

Peter D'Adamo further believes that blood types affect the personality. He claims that type O blood people are practical and organized. Type A's are more prone to stress. Type B's are a good cross between the O and A being more adaptable. Type AB is a cross between A and B.

# Blood Type O Diet

Peter D'Adamo in his book Eat Right for Your Type claims that following his diet suggestions help to lose weight by eating the right foods and avoiding the wrong foods. The American Academy of Family Physicians recommends for people to use caution with dieting and to make sure to consume well-balanced meals.

This book is specific to the blood type O diet, since type O is the most common. Peter D'Adamo believes that type O blood types are people full of energy. The diet suggested by D'Adamo suggests certain foods that help to build the energy and to reduce weight gain. Please note that all the statements made in this book follow along with the beliefs and suggestions made by Peter D'Adamo. Never take anyone's word about this, do the research for yourself before drawing your own conclusions. Just know that this book does follow with D'Adamo's beliefs and suggestions for the blood type diet plan.

Type Os do well eating a diet high in protein, especially meat. Type Os do not make good vegetarians. They need diets that include plenty of beef, cold-water fish, cod, tuna, rainbow trout, red snapper, halibut, swordfish, and salmon. Eat chicken and shellfish and almonds are okay to eat a couple times a week. A type O person can digest these easily because of the high acidity in their digestive systems.

Type O people often find they gain too much weight when eating foods that contain gluten and other whole grains. Type Os can eat barley and rice with no issues, but should substitute for wheat, corn, and oats.

Nuts such as pecans, pumpkin seeds and walnuts are beneficial to a type O. Some nuts like cashews, peanuts and pistachios and even kidney and navy beans, and lentils should be avoided, as they cause a greater production of stomach acid. Good legumes such as azuki beans, black-eyed peas, and pinto beans are safe to eat. Avoid eggs and egg products too.

Fruits are beneficial especially figs, cherries, prunes, and plums because they help the body to balance the digestive acidity. Citrus fruits like grapefruit, oranges, and tangerines are too high in acid for a type O. Other fruits to avoid are strawberries and blackberries. O blood types benefit from foods that promote thyroid health, because they tend to have more thyroid issues. Avoid these vegetables: Brussels sprouts, cabbage, cauliflower, eggplant and potatoes. Good vegetables are garlic, onions, peppers, pumpkin, okra, turnips, red peppers, leeks, beets, parsnips, Swiss chard, collard greens, and sweet potatoes. Fruits to consume in moderation are apples, grapes, melons, and bananas. Potatoes should be consumed in moderation, as we have found conflicting advice on potatoes for type O blood diet, some say to eat them daily while others say they are not beneficial. Perhaps good advice here would be to try it and see if it affects you in any way.

If you go on the blood type O diet you need to make sure you receive enough calcium and fiber, because the diet is lacking in the foods which naturally contain fiber and calcium. Type O negative needs to eat more chicken, turkey and venison, plus sea vegetables and fish to get the beneficial iodine nutrient. Everything else is the same.

# Blood Type A Diet

Type A blood does well on a vegetarian diet enjoying foods such as all vegetables and fruits including legumes and grains. They can eat seafood and soy protein. Foods to avoid are dairy food and red meat. Vegetables they need to avoid are cabbage, eggplant, peppers, potatoes and tomatoes. Type As need to practice exercises that calm and strengthen, much like yoga. This blood type needs to maintain a schedule of food intake, not skipping meals. They do well to eat their protein early in the day and sticking with more vegetables and fruit at night.

Type As do well to eat foods raw and unprocessed. Because they do not do well with animal proteins, they need to eat nuts, legumes, seeds, and tofu. Even though it is recommended to avoid dairy it is okay to consume mozzarella, ricotta, and yogurt in moderation.

# Blood Type B Diet

Type B blood, again, does well in the middle of type O and type A, enjoying a little of each foods. They are good to eat both animal protein and dairy. For weight loss, they should focus on eating plenty of eggs, liver, and vegetables. Foods like grains, nuts, and seeds may hinder weight loss, so eat these in moderation. Exercise is more like the type As have to practice, more of a calming but it is okay to do moderate exertion.

Type B's do well eating animal protein and can consume dairy without issues. They should include cottage cheese, cod, halibut, mackerel, milk, flounder, ocean perch, and salmon in their diet.

Vegetables suitable for type B are beets, cabbage, eggplants, bell peppers, broccoli, Brussels sprout, cauliflower, kale, jalapenos, carrots, yams, mustard greens, collard greens, and sweet potatoes.
Fruits suitable for type B are bananas, cranberries, grapes, pineapple, and plums. Type B needs to avoid avocados, coconuts, corn, and tomatoes. Spices to avoid are pepper, ketchup, almond extract, cinnamon, and allspice.

# Blood Type AB Diet

Type AB should follow a good cross section of type A and B. AB type can enjoy tofu, seafood, green vegetables, kelp, pineapple, green vegetables, rabbit, lamb, turkey, and mutton. Eggs can be eaten in moderation, a couple time a week, as well as soft dairy cheeses like cottage, mozzarella, and ricotta.

Foods to avoid include corn, polenta, beef, pork, venison, chicken, and buffalo. No pumpkin seeds, poppy seed or sunflower seeds either. No okra, tomatoes, pumpkin, onions, and turnips, either.
Why Wheat Free?

You will notice in these recipes that there is no call for any wheat food. The wheat grown and consumed thousands of years ago is not the same wheat we have today. Because of the interference with mutations and crossings, the wheat plant does not contain the same valuable nutrients it did in years past. Today there is a rise in the number of people suffering from "gluten intolerances and gluten allergies" because of the high protein content found in wheat today. Wheat causes the body to suffer with inflammation from the intolerances. Even tiny babies are showing wheat intolerances, according to a study by Pharmacia & Upjohn, a Diagnostics CAP System. Other studies show that close to 10 out of every 100 children has a wheat allergy. That is 10% of the population, and it is enough to take notice and do something about it. Avoiding wheat is the best place to start and that is why you will not find wheat ingredients within this recipe book.

# Blood Type Recipes

All the recipes in the Blood Type Diet book are inspired from recipes that have been around for a long time. While similar recipes may be found in books and on websites, all the recipes within this book are based on the blood type diet for O, A, B and AB as outlined by Peter D'Adamo in his books on blood type diet and his website as well.

# Blood Type O Recipes

## Appetizers and Snacks for Blood Type O

### Cheese Ball with Herbs

This recipe calls for a tofu cream cheese, but real cream cheese can be used, keeping in mind that dairy products need to be consumed in moderation only.

Makes 1 cheese ball.

***Ingredients:***

*1 cup of tofu cream cheese (or real cream cheese)
*1 1/2 tablespoon of parsley (dried)
*1 1/2 tablespoon of cilantro (fresh)
*1 tablespoon of chives (fresh snipped)
*2 teaspoons of onions (dried, minced)
*1/2 teaspoon of garlic (minced)
*1/4 teaspoon of thyme (dried)
*1/2 teaspoon of basil (dried)
*1/2 teaspoon of sage (dried)
*couple dashes of hot sauce

*pinch of salt

***Directions:***

In a bowl mix the 1 cup of tofu cream cheese (or real cream cheese) together with the 1 tablespoon of chives (fresh snipped), 2 teaspoons of onions (dried, minced), 1/2 teaspoon of garlic (minced), 1/4 teaspoon of thyme (dried), 1/2 teaspoon of basil (dried), 1/2 teaspoon of sage (dried), couple dashes of hot sauce, and a pinch of salt. With clean hand, shape into a ball. Mix the dried parsley and cilantro in a bowl then roll the ball in the 1 1/2 tablespoon of parsley (dried) and the 1 1/2 tablespoon of cilantro (fresh) until it is well coated. Cover and refrigerate for at least half an hour before serving. Serve with crackers.

## Spinach Dip with Artichokes

This dip is a must have for any party or gathering and goes perfectly with raw vegetables.

Makes a healthy party serving.

***Ingredients:***

*3 cups of spinach (fresh chopped)
*2 cups of vegetable stock
*1 3/4 cups of artichoke hearts
*1/2 cup of onion (diced)
*1/2 cup of mozzarella (shredded)
*1/3 cup of feta cheese
*1/4 cup of butter (clarified)
*1/4 cup of rice flour
*2 tablespoons of lemon juice
*1 teaspoon of salt
*1/2 teaspoon of garlic (dried)

***Directions:***

Heat the butter in a saucepan over medium heat. Add the 1/3 cup of diced onion and sauté. Stir in the 1/4 cup of rice flour, creating a nice roux. Pour in the 2 cups of vegetable stock, stirring as you pour. Increase the heat to medium high and stir until it thickens. Sprinkle in the 2 tablespoons of lemon juice, teaspoon of salt, and 1/2 teaspoon of powdered garlic and stir. Add the 3 cups of fresh chopped spinach, 1 3/4 cups of artichoke hearts, 1/2 cup of shredded mozzarella, and the 1/3 cup of feta cheese and stir over low heat until the cheese melts. Serve warm.

# Desserts and Treats for Blood Type O

## Sugar Cookies

These sugar cookies are gluten free.

Makes 2 dozen.

***Ingredients:***

*3/4 cup of rice flour (brown)
*1/2 cup of arrowroot flour
*1/2 cup of butter (clarified)
*1/4 cup of honey
*1 egg
*1 tablespoon of almond milk
*1/2 teaspoon of vanilla extract
*1/4 teaspoon of baking powder
*1/8 teaspoon of salt

***Directions:***

Prep: Preheat the oven to 350 degrees Fahrenheit. In a bowl, add the clarified butter along with the 1/4 cup of honey and the 1/8 teaspoon of salt, whipping it until it is light and fluffy. Stir in the egg, beating it well into the mixture. Add the tablespoon of almond milk and the 1/2 teaspoon of vanilla extract, stirring well. Last, in a separate bowl add the 3/4 cup of rice flour, 1/2 cup of arrowroot flour and the 1/4 teaspoon of baking powder and stir. Gradually stir into the batter. Drop by the teaspoonful's onto an ungreased cookie sheet, making sure they are at least an inch apart. Bake for about 9 minutes or until golden brown.

## Ginger Spice Cookies

This delicious ginger cook is gluten free.

Makes around 3 dozen cookies (depending on the size.)

***Ingredients:***

*3 cups of almond meal
*2 cups of flour (rice)
*1 cup of agave syrup
*4 eggs
*1 teaspoon of salt
*1 teaspoon of ginger (ground)
*1/2 teaspoon of cloves (ground)

***Directions:***

Prep: Preheat oven to 300 degrees Fahrenheit. Lightly spray a cookie sheet with cooking spray.

Add the 4 eggs to a bowl and beat. Then stir in the cup of agave syrup. In a separate bowl, add the 3 cups of almond meal, 2 cups of rice flour, teaspoon of salt, teaspoon of ground ginger, and 1/2 teaspoon of ground cloves. Pour the eggs and agave syrup into the dry ingredients and mix well. Drop by the teaspoonful onto the cookie sheet leaving at least 2 inches between each cookie. Bake in hot oven until golden brown, about 10 minutes. Allow to cool for 2 minutes on the cookie sheet before gently removing and placing on a wire rack for complete cooling. Enjoy immediately or store in a cookie jar or an airtight container.

# Breads and Rolls for Blood Type O

## Rye Bread

This is a lovely rye bread, perfect for eating alone or in a sandwich.

Makes 2 loaves.

***Ingredients:***

*7 1/2 cups of rye flour
*2 cups of water
*1 egg
*2 tablespoons of molasses
*1 tablespoon of yeast
*1 tablespoon of salt
*1/2 teaspoon of mustard (ground)
*1/4 teaspoon of onion powder

***Directions:***

Prep: Grease 2 loaf pans with cooking spray.

In a bowl add 7 1/2 cups of rye flour, 2 cups of water, 1 egg, 2 tablespoons of molasses, 1 tablespoon of yeast, 1 tablespoon of salt, 1/2 teaspoon of mustard (ground) and 1/4 teaspoon of onion powder and mix well. The dough will be thick. Spray a sheet of plastic wrap with cooking spray and loosely cover the bowl and place in a warm spot to rise. Allow it to rise to twice its original size and using your fist, punch it down, to release the air. Cover again and let it rise a second time, punching again and then divide the dough into two. Put into the 2 loaf pans and grease hands with butter or cooking spray and pat the dough into the bottom of the pans. Cover again with the sprayed plastic wrap and set in a warm spot for the final rise. Allow the dough to double its size. Before the dough fully reaches its size, preheat the oven to 350 degrees Fahrenheit. Grease a sharp knife and cut a slit down the center of each loaf at the top to make them a split top. Place the loaves in the hot oven and bake for about 40 minutes, until the top is a nice crisp brown.

## Dinner Rolls

These dinner rolls makes a great side dish with many entrees, and it is delicious with breakfast or as a quick snack too.

Makes 16 rolls.

***Ingredients:***

*3 cups of almond flour
*2 cups of flax (ground)
*1 cup of water
*6 eggs
*3 teaspoons of baking powder
*1 teaspoon of baking soda
*3/4 teaspoon of salt

***Directions:***

Prep: Preheat the oven to 350 degrees Fahrenheit. Spray 16 muffin tins with cooking spray. (Use 2 12-cup muffin pans)
Add the 3 cups of almond flour in a bowl along with the 2 cups of ground flax, 3 teaspoons of baking powder, teaspoon of baking soda and 3/4 teaspoon of salt and mix. Set aside, in a separate bowl add the 1 cup of water

with the 6 eggs, and beat. Gradually pour the egg water into the dry ingredient bowl and mix well. Set aside for 5 minutes, and then evenly spoon the batter into the 16 muffin tins. Bake until the tops turn a golden brown about 20 minutes. Allow to cool before removing from the pan.

# Main Dish Recipes for Blood Type O

## Meat Loaf

This is a delicious meat loaf made of turkey complete with a sauce topping.

Makes 4 servings.

***Ingredients:***

*1 1/2 pounds of turkey (ground white meat)
*1 cup of tomato paste
*1 cup of water
*1 cup of onion (sliced thin)
*1 cup of carrots (sliced thin)
*1/2 cup of onions (diced)
*4 seaweed leaves (roasted and ripped into tiny pieces)
*2 eggs (room temperature)
*1/4 teaspoon of garlic (minced)
*salt and pepper to taste

***Directions:***

Prep: Preheat oven to 400 degrees Fahrenheit. Spray a small loaf pan with cooking spray. (or use a special meat loaf pan with the drip tray)

Spray a non-stick frying pan with cooking spray and turn heat to medium. Add the cup of sliced thin onions and sliced thin carrots and sauté. Pour into a large bowl, add the 4 ripped seaweed leaves, and toss. Mix in the 1 1/2 pounds of white ground turkey. Beat the eggs in a cup and add to the meat mixture, with hands knead until mixed. Sprinkle salt and pepper. Add to the loaf pan. In a small bowl, mix the cup of tomato paste, cup of water, 1/2 cup of dice onions, and the 1/4 teaspoon of minced garlic. Poke holes in the top of the meatloaf with your finger and then pour the tomato sauce over the top, filling the holes and covering the top. Meat loaf is done when a meat thermometer inserted in the middle reads 165 degrees Fahrenheit. Start checking in 15 minutes, then check every 5 minutes. Allow to cool, turn out onto a platter and slice and serve.

## Chicken and Bean Stew

When the palate is craving a delicious comfort food, reach for this recipe and warm up to a hot steaming bowl of stew. This goes well with the Dinner Rolls.

Makes 4 servings.

***Ingredients:***

*2 cups of chicken broth
*1 1/2 cups of chicken breasts (cut into small chunks)
*1 1/2 cups of carrots (chopped)
*1 cup of water
*1 cup of beans (adzuki)
*1 cup of celery (chopped)
*3/4 cup of onions (sliced and cut)
*3 tablespoons of olive oil (divided)
*1 1/2 teaspoons of garlic (minced)
*1 bay leaf
*salt and pepper to taste

***Directions:***

Prep: Sort and wash the cup of adzuki beans and put in a bowl. Add enough water to cover the beans, about 1/2 inches above. Soak overnight.

Pour the water from the beans, add beans to a pot, and cover again with water. Place on stove on high temperature and bring to a boil. Turn down to low and cook for an hour, watching the water, making sure the beans stay covered in water. If you add more water, add hot water. Meanwhile, add the 2 tablespoons of olive oil to a skillet and turn heat to medium. Add the chunked chicken and cook until just done, careful not to "fry" it. Carefully remove the chicken from the skillet, placing it in a bowl, set aside. Keep the heat on the skillet at medium and add the final tablespoon of olive oil. Add the 3/4 cup of sliced cut onion and the 1 1/2 teaspoons of minced garlic and sauté. Place the 1 1/2 cups of chopped carrots and the cup of chopped celery in a small saucepan and cover with water. Place on high heat, bring to a boil, and boil for 5 minutes. Remove from heat and drain the water. In a large pan add the adzuki beans, browned chicken, sautéed onions and garlic, cooked carrots and celery, 2 cups of chicken broth, 1 cup of water, the bay leaf and salt and pepper. Bring to a quick boil on high heat, turn to low, and cook for about half an hour. Remove the bay leaf and allow cooling slightly before serving.

## Beef and Gravy

This makes a great dish to serve over steamed vegetables or rice.

Makes 6 servings.

***Ingredients:***

*2 pounds of beef (use whatever cut you like, slice into bite-sized cubes)
*1 3/4 cups of beef broth
*1/3 cup of rice flour
*1/4 cup of olive oil
*1/4 cup of onion (diced)
*2 tablespoons of Worcestershire sauce
*1 tablespoon of tamari
*1/2 teaspoon of pepper
*1/2 teaspoon of salt
*1/2 teaspoon of garlic (minced)

***Directions:***

Put the bite-sized beef in a large zipper bag along with the 1/3 cup of rice flour. Close the bag and shake to coat each piece of beef. Pour the 1/4 cup of olive oil in a skillet and heat to medium high, place the flour coated beef in the hot oil and brown the beef. Do this in batches so all pieces will be well done. Place on a platter and add the 1/4 cup of diced onion to the hot oil and the 1/2 teaspoon of mince garlic and sauté. If the oil is dried, pour in a little of the beef broth. Pour in the remainder of the beef broth once the onions are done along with the 2 tablespoons of Worcestershire sauce, tablespoon of tamari, 1/2 teaspoons of the pepper and salt. Turn the heat to low, cover and simmer for about 2 hours, or until the "gravy" is thick and bubbly. Pour the gravy over the beef, or add the beef and spoon it together to serve.

# Side Dish Recipes for Blood Type O

## Green Rice Stir Fry

This is an excellent side dish to go well with a meaty protein rich main dish.

Makes 2 large or 4 small servings.

***Ingredients:***

*1 cup of kale (chopped)
*3/4 cup of onion (red - chopped)
*3/4 cup of rice (basmati)
*1/2 cup of seaweed
*2 tablespoons of olive oil
*1 tablespoon of agave syrup
*1/2 tablespoon of turmeric
*1/4 tablespoon of coriander
*1/4 tablespoon of cayenne
*5 teaspoons of garlic (minced)

***Directions:***

Prep: Cook the 3/4 cup of basmati rice according to package directions.

Add the 2 tablespoons of olive oil to a frying pan and heat to medium. Stir in the 3/4 cup of chopped red onion, 1/2 cup of seaweed, and the 5 teaspoons of minced garlic and sauté. Add the 3/4 cup of cooked basmati rice with the tablespoon of agave syrup, 1/2 tablespoon of turmeric, 1/4 tablespoon of coriander and the 1/4 tablespoon of cayenne and continue cooking for another 10 minutes. Toss in the cup of chopped kale at the last minute, and stir until wilted. Serve immediately with a meat main dish.

## Potato Salad

Potato salad goes with many meat dishes.

Makes 4 servings.

***Ingredients:***

*8 cups of potatoes (cubed)
*2 cups of celery (sliced)
*2 cups of mayonnaise
*1 cup of onion (minced
*4 eggs
*4 tablespoons of vinegar
*3 teaspoons of salt
*2 teaspoons of sugar
*1/2 teaspoon of pepper

***Directions:***

Prep: Boil the 4 eggs to "hard boiled." Cook the 8 cups of potatoes until tender enough to eat, but not mashed.

In a small bowl, mix the 2 cups of mayonnaise, 4 tablespoons of vinegar, 3 teaspoons of salt, 2 teaspoons of sugar, and 1/2 teaspoon of pepper. In a large bowl, add the 4 minced hard-boiled eggs along with the 8 cups of cooked cubed potatoes, 2 cups of sliced celery, and the cup of minced onion. Toss, then pour the mayonnaise mixture and gently stir to coat well. Serve with meal.

# Blood Type A Recipes

## Appetizers and Snacks

### Sardine Salad Spread

This delicious spread is great on crackers or bread.

Makes 2 sandwiches or spread for 8 crackers.

***Ingredients:***

*2 cans of sardines (water packed 8 oz.)
*juice from one lemon
*1 cup of onions (diced)
*1 cup of bell pepper (diced)
*4 tablespoons of tahini
*2 tablespoons of olive oil
*4 teaspoons of garlic (minced)
*2 teaspoons of cumin
*1 teaspoon of salt

***Directions:***

Open the 2 cans of sardines and drain the water. Add to a bowl and mash. Mix in the 4 tablespoons of tahini, 4 teaspoons of minced garlic, 2 teaspoons of cumin and the teaspoon of salt. Heat the 2 tablespoons of olive oil in a skillet over medium heat. Add the cup of diced onions and the cup of diced bell pepper and sauté. Mix the vegetables in with the mashed sardines. Stir in the juice of the lemon. Refrigerate until chilled then spread on bread or crackers.

## Fried Asparagus

Fried asparagus makes great appetizers and may be used in place of French fries as well.

Makes 4 servings.

***Ingredients:***

*16 sprigs of asparagus
*olive oil
*salt

***Directions:***

Prep: Line a baking sheet with foil. Preheat the oven to broil.

Cut the asparagus for cooking by snipping the ends. Lay the asparagus on the lined baking sheet, drizzle with olive oil then sprinkle with salt. Place under the broiler for 8 minutes. Turn the asparagus sprigs over and bake for another 4 minutes. Enjoy.

# Desserts and Treats for Blood Type A

## Blue-Cranberry Muffins

A delicious muffin that is good as a dessert or even for breakfast or brunch.

Makes 2 dozen muffins.

***Ingredients:***

*3 cups of flour (spelt)
*1 1/2 cups of blueberries (frozen)
*1 1/2 cups of cranberries (chopped)
*1 cup of olive oil
*1 cup of honey
*4 eggs
*4 teaspoons of lime juice
*1 1/2 teaspoons of baking soda
*1 teaspoon of vanilla

***Directions:***

Prep: Preheat oven to 350 degrees Fahrenheit. Line 24 muffin tins with cupcake liners.

Add the 3 cups of spelt flour to a bowl along with the 1 1/2 teaspoons of baking soda and mix. Set aside. In a separate bowl, add the 4 eggs and beat, then add the cup of olive oil, cup of honey, 4 teaspoons of lime juice and the teaspoon of vanilla. Mix well, and gradually add in the dry ingredients. Equally spoon the batter into the 24 lined muffin tins. Bake until tops turn a golden brown, about 25 minutes.

## Fudge Cookies

This delicious recipe for cookies calls for carob instead of cocoa and non-wheat flours.

Makes 3 dozen cookies.

***Ingredients:***

*1 3/4 cups of flour (spelt)
*1/2 cup of carob powder
*1/2 cup of walnuts (chopped)
*1/2 cup of honey
*1/2 cup of soy milk
*1/3 cup of olive oil
*1 1/2 teaspoons of baking powder
*1/4 teaspoon of salt

***Directions:***

Prep: Preheat the oven to 350 degrees Fahrenheit.

Mix the 1 3/4 cups of spelt flour with the 1/2 cup of carob powder, 1 1/2 teaspoons of baking powder, and the 1/4 teaspoon of salt. In a separate bowl, add the1/2 cup of honey, 1/2 cup of soy milk, 1/3 cup of olive oil and stir. Gradually add the dry ingredients, and then gently fold in the 1/2 cup of chopped walnuts. Drop by the teaspoonful onto an ungreased baking sheet. Bake for 8 minutes. Allow to cool for 2 minutes on the cookie sheet before transferring to a wire rack for complete cooling.

# Breads and Rolls for Blood Type A

## Rice Bread

This is a delicate light bread that goes well with meals.

Makes one round loaf.

***Ingredients:***

*1 cup of flour (rice)
*1 cup of soy milk
*2 eggs
*2 teaspoons of baking powder
*1 teaspoon of basil (dried)
*1 teaspoon of oregano (dried)
*1/4 teaspoon of salt

***Directions:***

Prep: Add the cup of rice flour in a bowl along with the cup of soy milk and sit for an hour. Next in a separate bowl, add just the egg whites reserving the yolks. With a whisk beat the egg whites until peaks form. Add the rice flour and milk mixture to the egg whites and gently stir. Mix in the 2 egg yolks along with the 2 teaspoons of baking powder, teaspoon of dried basil, teaspoon of dried oregano and the 1/4 teaspoon of salt. Next, spray the top of a double boiler with cooking spray and place the dough in the top of it. Cover the top with foil, making a tent to allow the bread to rise as it cooks. Set the stove to produce a gentle boil in the pan of water beneath the bread. Make sure the foil covers the bread not to allow water to get into the top pan. Allow the water to boil gently for 80 minutes under the bread pan. Remove the pan from the double boiler and let it cool on a wire rack for about 10 minutes. Turn out onto a platter and allow cooling completely. Serve immediately, or store in an airtight container for a couple of days.

## Buttermilk Biscuits

Biscuits go well with any meal from breakfast through supper.
Makes a dozen biscuits.

***Ingredients:***

*2 cups of flour (spelt)
*1 cup of buttermilk
*1 tablespoon of baking powder
*1/4 teaspoon of salt

***Directions:***

Prep: Preheat oven to 425 degrees Fahrenheit. Lightly spray a baking sheet with cooking spray.

Add the 2 cup of spelt flour along with the tablespoon of baking powder and 1/4 teaspoon of salt to a bowl and mix. Stir in the cup of buttermilk. Evenly drop by spoonful's onto the baking sheet making a dozen biscuits. Bake until golden brown, around 13 minutes.

## Main Dish Recipes Side Dish Recipes for Blood Type A

### Italian Chicken Breasts

This chicken dish makes an Italian treat that all will love.

Makes 6 servings.

***Ingredients:***

*6 chicken breast halves (boneless and skinless)
*1 cup of bread crumbs (fine)
*1/4 cup of Romano cheese (grated)
*3 tablespoons of oregano (dried)
*2 tablespoons of kelp (powder)

***Directions:***

Prep: Preheat oven to 375 degrees Fahrenheit. In a shallow dish, mix the cup of fine breadcrumbs with the 1/4 cup of grated Romano cheese, 3 tablespoons of dried oregano, and the 2 tablespoons of kelp powder. Rinse the chicken breast halves, and then roll through the breadcrumb mixture. Arrange the breasts in a baking dish, not overlapping. Bake for about an hour, checking to make sure the temperature reaches 165 degrees Fahrenheit with a meat thermometer inserted into the middle.

## Salmon with Eggplant

Salmon is so beneficial, chocked full of nutrients. Try this delicious dish, which features eggplant.

Makes 4 servings.

***Ingredients:***

*1 pound of salmon (fillet - skinless)
*1/2 cup of basil leaves (fresh)
*1/2 cup of olive oil (extra virgin)
*10 parsley sprigs (fresh)
*3 tablespoons of pine nuts
*1 tablespoon of garlic (minced) +1 teaspoon
*1 teaspoon of olive oil
*salt to taste

***Directions:***

Prep: Preheat the oven to 350 degrees Fahrenheit.

Cut the salmon fillets into 4 servings. Rinse with water and dry with a paper towel. Place the salmon fillets in a glass baking dish and sprinkle the teaspoon of olive oil along with the tablespoon of minced garlic. Make the pesto by adding these ingredients into a food processor or blender: 3 tablespoons of pine nuts and 1 teaspoon of minced garlic. Chop the two ingredients. Add the 1/2 cup of fresh basil leaves, 10 fresh parsley sprigs and the 1/2 cup of extra virgin olive oil and continue to "chop" until it forms pesto. Sprinkle with salt to taste. Spread the pesto over the top of the salmon. Bake in the oven for 15 minutes, uncovered. Serve immediately.

## Green Pasta Dish

This is a perfect dish for vegetarians as well as all blood types, especially type A.

Makes 4 servings.

***Ingredients:***

*1 pound of artichoke pasta
*1 pound of raw spinach (washed and chopped)
*1 bunch of Swiss chard (washed and chopped and trimmed)
*1 cup of leeks (sliced)
*1/4 cup of olive oil
*1 teaspoon of garlic (minced)
*salt to taste
*Romano cheese to taste

***Directions:***

Pour water in a large pot and bring to a boil on the stove. Add the artichoke pasta and cook according to package directions. In a large frying pan add the 1/4 cup of olive oil and cook the cup of sliced leeks until they tenderize. Add the teaspoon of minced garlic and cook for another minute. Toss in the pound of raw spinach and the bunch of Swiss chard and cook until the greens wilt and are fully cooked through. Toss in some salt and Romano cheese and serve.

# Side Dish Recipes for Blood Type A

## Spicy Beets and Vegetables

This side dish gives beneficial nutrients from the beets, carrots, and turnips.

Makes 4 servings.

***Ingredients:***

*6 beets (greens included, peeled and cubed)
*2 turnips (fresh. peeled and cubed)
*4 cups of carrots (chopped)
*1/2 cup of onion (yellow chopped)
*2 tablespoons of tamari
*1/2 teaspoon of allspice
*1/2 teaspoon of cinnamon (ground)
*1/4 teaspoon of ginger (ground)
*1/4 teaspoon of cloves
*olive oil
*salt to taste

***Directions:***

Add the 6 chopped and peeled beets along with the 4

cups of chopped carrots to a pot of boiling water. Salt the water. Boil for 10 minutes to soften. Drain the water and set to the side. Add a little olive oil to a skillet and turn to medium heat, add the 1/2 cup of chopped yellow onion and sauté. Add the 2 peeled and cubed turnips along with the 2 tablespoons of tamari, 1/2 teaspoon of allspice, 1/2 teaspoon of ground cinnamon, 1/4 teaspoon of ground ginger, and the 1/4 teaspoon of cloves. Sauté for another 5 minutes. Pour in the beet and carrot mixture and continue cooking for another 7 minutes. Salt to taste.

## Rice Stuffing

This is an excellent side dish to turkey or chicken.

Makes about 4 servings.

***Ingredients:***

*2 cup of rice (cooked)
*1/2 cup of celery (chopped, celery leaves included)
*1/4 cup of onion (chopped)
*1 tablespoon of parsley (dried)
*1 tablespoon of poultry seasoning (add more if desired)
*salt to taste
*olive oil

***Directions:***

Pour enough olive oil to coat the bottom of a skillet and heat to medium. Add the 1/2 cup of chopped celery and celery leaves with the 1/4 cup of chopped onion). Sprinkle in the tablespoon of dried parsley and the poultry seasoning. Stir in the rice and add extra olive oil if needed to keep it moist. Salt to taste. Stir until heated through.

# Blood Type B Recipes

## Appetizers and Snacks for Blood Type B

### Potato Chips

These are not your average potato chips, they are made from sweet potatoes.

Makes 4 servings.

***Ingredients:***

*4 sweet potatoes (sliced very thin)
*salt to taste
*cayenne pepper to taste

***Directions:***

Prep: Preheat oven to 450 degrees. Spray a cookie sheet with cooking spray. (may need 2 cookie sheets)
Spread the sweet potato slices on a single layer on the sprayed cookie sheet. Bake until the slices turn golden and crisp. It only takes a couple of minutes. Sprinkle salt

and cayenne pepper while hot, serve immediately. Store in an airtight container. May spread and reheat for 2 minutes after storage.

## Meatballs a la Turkey

Meatballs make a great appetizer, just skewer with a toothpick, place on a platter and you have a hit.

Makes 2 pounds of meatballs.

***Ingredients:***

*2 pounds of turkey (ground)
*1 cup of bread crumbs
*1 cup of cranberries (dried and chopped)
*1/2 cup of onion (minced)
*1/2 cup of parsley (fresh chopped)
*1 1/2 teaspoon of garlic (minced)
*salt to taste
*pepper to taste

***Directions:***

Prep: Preheat oven to 400 degrees Fahrenheit. Spray a broiler pan with cooking spray.

In a large bowl add the 2 pounds of turkey, then add the 1 cup of bread crumbs, 1 cup of cranberries, dried and chopped), 1/2 cup of onion (minced), 1/2 cup of parsley (fresh chopped), 1 1/2 teaspoon of garlic (minced), salt to taste, and the pepper to taste. With hands, mix all the ingredients well. Shape into 1-inch meatballs. Place on the greased broiler pan and back until the tops brown, turn the meatballs and brown on all sides. Serve with toothpicks and dip into favorite dipping sauce, or with pasta and sauce.

# Desserts and Treats for Blood Type B

## Chocolate Chip Cookies

Most people enjoy a good chocolate chip cookie, these are very good.

Makes 2 dozen cookies.

***Ingredients:***

*2 cups of rice flour (brown)
*1 cup of honey
*1 cup of canola oil
*1/2 cup of potato flour
*1/2 cup of water
*1/2 cup of chocolate chips
*2 eggs
*4 teaspoons of baking powder
*2 teaspoons of vanilla extract
*1 teaspoon of baking soda
*2 dashes of stevia

***Directions:***

Prep: Preheat oven to 375 degrees Fahrenheit.

Add the 2 eggs to a large bowl and beat and then add in the 1 cup of honey, 1 cup of canola oil, 2 teaspoons of vanilla extract, and the 2 dashes of stevia and stir well. In a separate bowl, mix the 2 cups of brown rice flour, 1/2 cup of potato flour, 4 teaspoons of baking powder, and the teaspoon of baking soda. Gradually add the dry ingredients into the batter. Fold in the 1/2 cup of chocolate chips. Using greased hands make 2 dozen balls and place on a cookie sheet 2 inches apart. Bake in oven for about 11 minutes, until light golden brown. Allow to cool on pan for 2 minutes, then remove to wire rack until completely cooled.

## CranNut Cake

This is a delicious small cake, perfect to satisfy the sweet tooth.
Makes one 13x9 or two98 inch round cakes.

***Ingredients:***

*2 cups of rice flour
*2 cups of flax meal
*2 cups of hot water
*2 cups of cranberries
*2 cups of walnuts
*1 1/4 cup of honey
*2 tablespoons of ghee
*2 tablespoons of black strap molasses
*2 teaspoons of baking soda
*1 teaspoon of cloves

***Directions:***

Prep: Preheat oven to 350 degrees Fahrenheit. Spray the baking pan(s) with cooking spray.

In a bowl mix the 2 cups of rice flour, 2 cups of flax meal with the 2 cups of hot water. Stir and set aside for 10 minutes. In a separate bowl add the 1 1/4 cup of honey,

2 tablespoons of ghee, 2 tablespoons of black strap molasses, 2 teaspoons of baking soda, and the teaspoon of cloves and stir. Mix in the flours and water bowl. Fold in the 2 cups each of the cranberries and the walnuts. If you desire, chop the cranberries and nuts first. Pour the thick batter into the prepared pan(s) and bake for around 25 minutes, until the top turns a nice golden brown. You may frost with your favorite frosting.

# Breads and Rolls for Blood Type B

## Loaf of Bread

This is a great bread to slice and eat with sandwiches or to make toast.

Makes one loaf of bread.

***Ingredients:***

*1 cup of hot water
*1 cup of cannellini bean flour
*1 cup of rice flour (brown)
*3/4 cup of almond milk
*1/2 cup of flax meal
*1/2 cup of arrowroot
*3 eggs
*3 tablespoons of olive oil
*1 tablespoon of vinegar (apple cider)
*1 tablespoon of honey + 1 teaspoon
*1 tablespoon of yeast
*2 teaspoons of lecithin
*1 1/2 teaspoon of salt

***Directions:***

Prep: Heat the oven to 200 degrees Fahrenheit, then turn the oven off and leave the oven door open just a touch to allow the heat to escape.

Add the teaspoon of honey and the tablespoon of honey to the cup of hot water, stir, and set aside. Add the cups of cannellini bean flour, brown rice flour, 1/2 cup of flax meal, 1/2 cup of arrowroot, 2 teaspoons of lecithin, and 1 1/2 teaspoons of salt to a bowl and stir. In a separate bowl beat the 3 eggs and add the 3/4 cup of almond milk, 3 tablespoons of olive oil, tablespoon of apple cider vinegar, and the tablespoon of honey and stir well. Gradually add the dry ingredients into the wet ingredients, including the yeast and honey water. Beat with an electric beater for one minute. Prepare the loaf pan by spraying with cooking spray and place a sheet of parchment paper in the bottom. Place the dough in the prepared loaf pan. Place a towel over the loaf pan and place the pan in the oven to let it rise for about an hour. The loaf is ready when it rises just over the top of the loaf pan. Remove the cloth and turn the oven to 350 degrees Fahrenheit. Bake until the top turns a nice golden brown, about 45 minutes.

## Dinner Rolls for Type B

These rolls make a delicious bread side dish for many meals.

Makes 15 rolls.

***Ingredients:***

*6 cups of spelt flour (white)
*2 cups of warm water (just shy of 2 cups, a smidgen less)
*1/3 cup of cold water
*3 teaspoons of yeast
*1 1/2 tablespoons of honey
*1 1/2 tablespoons of olive oil
*1 3/4 teaspoons of salt
*1 1/2 teaspoon of arrowroot

***Directions:***

Add the 6 cups of white spelt flour with the 3 teaspoons of yeast, and the 1 3/4 teaspoons of salt, and stir in the "just shy of" 2 cups of warm water, 1 1/2 tablespoons of honey, and the 1 1/2 tablespoons of olive oil. Line a baking sheet (or two) with parchment paper. With greased hands make 15 oval shaped "rolls" and place on the parchment paper with about 2 inches between each roll. Spray a piece of plastic wrap with cooking spray and loosely cover the rolls. Set aside to rise to desired size, about an hour. Preheat oven to 350 degrees Fahrenheit. Remove the plastic wrap (carefully). Mix the 1 1/2 teaspoons of arrowroot into the 1/3 cup of cold water. Brush the tops of the rolls with the mixture. Place the rolls in the hot oven and bake until golden brown, around half an hour.

# Main Dish Recipes for Blood Type B

## Fried Chicken Steak

This is a delicious main entree.

Makes 4 servings.

***Ingredients:***

*1 pound of beef cube steak
*1/2 cup of spelt flour
*1/4 cup of soy milk
*1 egg
*2 tablespoons of olive oil (extra virgin)
*garlic salt to taste
*crushed red peppers to taste

***Directions:***

Add the 2 tablespoons of olive oil to a skillet and heat to medium high. In a shallow bowl add the egg and beat, then add the soy milk and mix well with a whisk. In a separate shallow bowl add the 1/2 cup of spelt flour and sprinkle with the garlic salt and crushed red peppers. Cut the beef cube steak into four equal portions. Dip each piece of beef cube steak into the egg mixture, then drag through the flour mixture and place in the skillet and cook for at least 3 minutes. Turn over and cook an additional three minutes.

## Steak and Mushrooms

Here is another great recipe using your favorite cut of lean steak.

Makes 2 large servings or 4 small servings.

***Ingredients:***

*1 to 2 pounds of steak (your favorite cut, lean)
*2 cups of greens (mustard, turnip, broccoli, etc. your choice)
*1 cup of carrots (chopped)
*1 cup of vegetable broth
*1 cup of Portobello mushrooms (chopped)
*1/4 cup of parsley (fresh minced)
*2 tablespoons of lime juice
*2 tablespoons of olive oil
*1 tablespoon of pine nuts
*1 tablespoon of rice flour
*1 tablespoon of garlic (minced)
*1 tablespoon of honey
*1 teaspoon of mustard (prepared)
*salt to taste
*pepper to taste

***Directions:***

Put the 2 cups of greens and the chopped cup of carrots into a steamer and let them steam while preparing the rest. Cook the steak in your favorite method (grill, broiler, frying pan) and salt and pepper. Add the 2 tablespoons of olive oil to a skillet and heat to medium. Add the tablespoon of minced garlic and the cup of chopped Portobello mushrooms and sauté. Stir in the tablespoon of rice flour to make a rue. Pour in the cup of vegetable broth, stirring as you pour. Add the 2 tablespoons of lime juice, tablespoon of honey and teaspoon of prepared mustard, stirring while the gravy thickens. Add salt and pepper if desired. Put the dish together by spooning a serving of vegetables on the plate; place the cooked meat on top of the steamed vegetables. Pour the gravy over the meat. Garnish with a sprinkling of fresh minced parsley and a few pine nuts. Add more salt and pepper and enjoy.

## Baked Italian Meatballs

This is a delicious main course that goes well with pasta and vegetables.

Makes 6 servings.

***Ingredients:***

*2 pounds of ground beef (lean)
*1 cup of bread crumbs (fine)
*1/2 cup of Romano cheese (pecorino)
*1/2 cup of parsley (fresh chopped)
*1/4 cup of soy milk
*2 eggs
*1 tablespoon of basil leaf (dried)
*3 teaspoons of garlic (minced)
*salt to taste
*pepper to taste

***Directions:***

Prep: Preheat the oven to 350 degrees Fahrenheit.

Beat the 2 eggs then add to a large bowl along with the remaining ingredients. With hands, combine the 2 pounds of ground beef (lean),1 cup of bread crumbs (fine), 1/2 cup of Romano cheese (pecorino), 1/2 cup of parsley (fresh chopped), 1/4 cup of soy milk, 1 tablespoon of basil leaf (dried), and the 3 teaspoons of garlic (minced). Salt and pepper the mixture and combine well. Roll the meat mixture into whatever size meatballs you want. The larger they are the longer it takes to cook. Line a baking sheet with foil and place the meatballs in a single layer. Bake in the oven for 20 to 30 minutes, turning the meatballs every 5 to 10 minutes to brown on all sides.

# Side Dish Recipes for Blood Type B

## Roasted Sweet Potatoes

Sweet potatoes go well with so many different main entrees. They also make a great sweet snack.

Makes 4 servings.

***Ingredients:***

*2 sweet potatoes (cut in half lengthwise)
*1/4 cup of olive oil
*salt to taste

***Directions:***

Prep: Preheat the oven to 400 degrees Fahrenheit. Cover a baking sheet with foil.

Brush the oil over the tops of the sweet potato halves and sprinkle with salt. Bake for half an hour, the peel will be crisp and the top a golden brown.

## Green Beets

Do not let the name full you, the green means the tops of the beets, but the meat of the beets are still a deep red. This is a wonderful side dish that goes well with so many foods, it also acts as a soup.

Makes 4 servings.

***Ingredients:***

*4 cups of beets and greens (washed and chopped greens, thin sliced beets)
*2 cups of vegetable broth
*4 tablespoons of olive oil

***Directions:***

In a stockpot, pout the 4 tablespoons of olive oil and heat to medium high. Stir in the beets until heated, stir in the greens, and then add the 2 cups of vegetable broth. Cover and continue to simmer until the beets are tender enough to eat.

# Blood Type AB Recipes

## Appetizers and Snacks for Blood Type AB

### Tortilla Cracker Chips

Everyone deserves a chippy or cracker snack, to eat with your favorite spread or dip. These can be both.

Makes 4 servings. (more or less depending on how many you want to eat in one sitting, because these are so good you cannot have just one!)

***Ingredients:***

*2 cups of amaranth flour
*6 tablespoons of water (or more)
*2 tablespoons of olive oil
*salt to taste

***Directions:***

Prep: Preheat oven to 350 degrees Fahrenheit.

Pour the 2 cups of amaranth flour into a bowl and add the 6 tablespoons of water to form a nice dough. Add more water if needed. With hands (grease with olive oil if needed or pat with amaranth flour) form into a dough ball. Divide into eight portions. Place the dough balls onto a floured surface and roll into flat "tortillas". Keep the rolling pin floured as well as the surface. Place 4 tortillas onto two baking sheets. Brush the olive oil on the tops of the tortillas. Sprinkle with salt. Bake until the tortillas are a golden brown and crisp like a cracker or chip, about 7 minutes.

## Veggies and Goat's Cheese Dip

This is a great dip for that tortilla cracker chips recipe or for any sliced or diced raw vegetable.

Makes a little over a cup (enough to put in a bowl and enjoy at a small dinner party or to eat alone!)

***Ingredients:***

*1 cup of goat's cheese
*2 tablespoons of lemon juice
*2 tablespoons of parsley (dried)
*1 tablespoon of sour cream
*1 teaspoon of ginger (ground)
*1 teaspoon of coriander (ground)
*1/2 teaspoon of garlic (minced)
*dash of paprika

***Directions:***

Prep: Allow the goat's cheese to warm up to room temperature.

Add the cup of goat's cheese to a bowl, pour the 2 tablespoons of lemon juice in, and mash the cheese and juice together. Add the 2 tablespoons of dried parsley, tablespoon of sour cream, teaspoon of ground ginger, teaspoon of ground coriander, and the 1/2 teaspoon of minced garlic and mix well. Sprinkle paprika over the top and serve with raw vegetables, crackers, or chips.

# Desserts and Treats for Blood Type AB

## Coffee Cake

This cake makes a wonderful dessert but can make a great breakfast and snack too.

Makes one 8x8 square or 8 inch round cake.

***Ingredients:***

*1 cup of millet flour
*1 1/4 cup of rice flour (brown) (divided)
*3/4 cup of water + more as needed
*1/3 cup of rice flour (sweet)
*1/4 cup of water (boiling hot)
*1/4 cup of almonds (ground)
*1 packet of yeast
*3 tablespoons of olive oil
*4 tablespoons of agave syrup (divided)
*1 tablespoon of flax meal (golden)
*1 tablespoon of lemon juice
*2 teaspoons of canola oil
*1/2 teaspoon of baking soda
*3/4 teaspoon of salt (divided)

***Directions:***

Prep: Preheat oven to 350 degrees Fahrenheit. Lightly spray an 8x8 or 8-inch round pan with cooking spray.

In a bowl, combine 1 cup of millet flour, 1 cup of brown rice flour, 1/3 cup of sweet rice flour, and the packet of yeast. In a separate bowl, combine the 3/4 cup of water, 3 tablespoons of olive oil, 2 tablespoons of agave syrup, and the tablespoon of lemon juice. Add the tablespoon of golden flax meal to the 1/4 cup of boiling water. Pour the water, flax meal into the wet ingredients and stir. Gently add the dry ingredients into the batter and stir. Pour the batter into the prepared pan. In a small bowl, combine the 1/4 cup of ground almonds, 1/4 cup of rice flour, 2 tablespoons of agave syrup, and the 2 teaspoons of canola oil. Sprinkle over the top of the batter in the pan do not stir. Bake until the top turns a golden brown, about 20 minutes.

## Nutty Baked Yellow Delicious Apples

For apple lovers this is a delicious apple desert.

Makes 4 servings.

***Ingredients:***

*4 yellow delicious apples (large)
*1 cup of apple juice
*1 cup of yogurt (plain)
*1/2 cup of almond butter (creamy)
*1/3 cup of raisins
*1 tablespoon of honey
*1 1/2 teaspoons of vanilla extract
*1/2 teaspoon of cinnamon (ground)
*1/4 teaspoon of nutmeg (ground)

***Directions:***

Prep: Preheat oven to 375 degrees Fahrenheit.

In a bowl, combine the 1/2 cup of creamy almond butter, 1/3 cup of raisins, 1 1/2 teaspoons of vanilla extract, 1/2 teaspoon of ground cinnamon, 3/4 tablespoon of apple juice with the 1/4 teaspoon of ground nutmeg. Carefully cut the core from the top of the apple, leaving the bottom intact, creating a narrow bowl inside the apple. Fill each apple with the almond butter mixture. Place the 4 apples in a baking dish. Pour the remainder from the cup of apple juice into the dish. Carefully place in the oven and bake for 20 minutes. While baking, mix the cup of plain yogurt with the tablespoon of honey. To serve place a baked apple on a plate or shallow bowl and drizzle the yogurt sauce over the top.

# Breads and Rolls for Blood Type AB

## Zucchini Bread

This is your classic zucchini bread that can be a dessert or as a sweet part of the main meal.

Makes 2 loaves.

***Ingredients:***

*2 cups of rice flour
*2 cups of flax meal (golden)
*2 cups of zucchini (shredded)
*1 cup of raisins
*1 cup of apple juice (thawed out from frozen concentrate, not diluted)
*1 cup of hot water
*1/2 cup of yogurt
*1 tablespoon of vanilla extract
*2 teaspoons of baking soda
*1 teaspoon of salt
*1 teaspoon of cinnamon (ground)

***Directions:***

Prep: Preheat oven to 350 degrees Fahrenheit. Spray 2 loaf pans with cooking spray.

In a bowl, combine the 2 cups of rice flour, 2 cups of golden flax meal, 2 teaspoons of baking soda, 1 teaspoon of salt with the teaspoon of ground cinnamon. In a separate bowl, combine the cup thawed apple juice concentrate with the cup of hot water, 1/2 cup of yogurt, and the tablespoon of vanilla extract. Stir in the 2 cups of shredded zucchini and the cup of raisins. Gradually add the dry ingredients and mix well. Divide between the 2 loaf pans and back for a little over an hour. Cool completely in pan before removing.

## Bagels

These bagels are good by themselves or as a sandwich for breakfast, lunch or supper or as a bread with a full meal.

Makes a dozen bagels.

***Ingredients:***

*2 cups of spelt flour (whole)
*2 cups of spelt flour (white)
*1 cup of milk
*1 packet of yeast
*2 eggs - divided
*1 tablespoon of salt + 1 teaspoon
*1 tablespoon of olive oil
*1 teaspoon of sugar

***Directions:***

Pour the milk into a saucepan and heat to luke warm. Stir in the packet of yeast. In a bowl, add the yeast milk along with 1 egg, and 1 tablespoon of olive oil and mix. In a separate bowl, mix the 2 cups of whole spelt flour with the 2 cups of white spelt flour and the teaspoon of salt and teaspoon of sugar. Mix in with the wet ingredients to form the dough. Cover the bowl with a cloth and allow rising for about 45 minutes. Preheat the oven to 400 degrees Fahrenheit. Sprinkle a flat surface with flour and coat your hands with flour, pour the dough onto the floured surface and "knead" the dough. Pull apart into a dozen lumps. Roll each dough lump into a rope and form a "ring" the size of a bagel. Add water to a large pot and add the tablespoon of salt. Bring the water to a boil and drop in the bagels, doing one at a time. Boil for 2 minutes. Beat the remaining egg. Remove the bagel and put on a baking sheet. Do this for every bagel. Brush each bagel with the beaten egg. Bake in the preheated oven until golden brown, about 17 minutes.

# Main Dish Recipes for Blood Type AB

## Chicken Curry

This dish is a one dish meal, or have other side dishes with it.

Makes 4 servings.

***Ingredients:***

*5 cups of potatoes (quartered)
*3 cups of tomatoes (canned, chopped)
*2 chicken breasts (skinned, boneless and chunked)
*2 cups of onions (chopped)
*1/2 teaspoon of garlic (minced)
*1 bay leaf
*1 vegetable bullion
*1/8 teaspoon of cumin (ground)
*1/8 teaspoon of ginger (ground)
*1/8 teaspoon of paprika
*1/8 teaspoon of cayenne chili pepper
*1/8 teaspoon of turmeric
*olive oil
*salt and pepper

***Directions:***

Add a little olive oil to a skillet and turn to medium heat. Add the 2 chunked chicken breasts and cook until white. Put the cooked chicken along with the 5 cups of potatoes (quartered), 3 cups of tomatoes (canned, chopped), 2 cups of onions (chopped), 1/2 teaspoon of garlic (minced), 1 vegetable bullion, 1/8 teaspoon of cumin (ground), 1/8 teaspoon of ginger (ground), 1/8 teaspoon of paprika, 1/8 teaspoon of cayenne chili pepper, 1/8 teaspoon of turmeric and the dashes of salt and pepper and stir. Add the bay leaf. Pour enough hot water to cover the food with about an inch over the top. Turn heat to high and stir while it cooks for 15 minutes. Turn heat to low and simmer, covered, for another 15 minutes. Stir often. Dish is done when the potatoes are soft and tender.

## Turkey Burgers

These great burgers work well as a sandwich or as a meat with the main meal.

Makes 4 servings.

***Ingredients:***

*1 pound of turkey (ground)
*1/2 cup of water
*1 teaspoon of lemon zest
*1 teaspoon of chicken broth
*1 teaspoon of lemon juice
*1/2 teaspoon of sage
*1/2 teaspoon of salt
*1/2 teaspoon of ginger (ground)
*couple dashes of hot sauce

***Directions:***

Add the turkey in a bowl and combine with the 1/2 cup of water, teaspoon of lemon zest, teaspoon of chicken broth, teaspoon of lemon juice and the dashes of hot sauce. In a cup add the 1/2 teaspoons of ground ginger, sage and salt and mix, then sprinkle into the turkey, and with hands mix well. Form into 4 quarter pound patties and cook until well done in a frying pan, grill or under the broiler, about 7 minutes on each side.

## Savory Chicken and Wild Rice

This main dish recipe features the wholesome goodness of wild rice with savory herbs and mushrooms to make it as filling, as it is delicious.

Makes 4 servings.

***Ingredients:***

* 1 1/2 pounds of ground chicken
*4 cups of maitake mushrooms (sliced)
*2 1/2 cups of water
*1 cup of wild rice
*1 1/2cup of chicken broth
*1/2 cup of onion (chopped)
*1/2 cup of celery (chopped)
*2 tablespoons of cornstarch
*2 tablespoons of soy sauce
*1 tablespoon of parsley flakes
*1 tablespoon of basil (dried)
*1 teaspoon of oregano (ground)
*1/2 teaspoon of sage (ground)
*1/2 teaspoon of marjoram
*1/2 teaspoon of rosemary

***Directions:***

Pour 2 cups of water into a saucepan, add the wild rice, and bring to a boil on high heat. Cover the pan, turn to low, and simmer for 45 minutes. After the rice is cooked place a non-stick skillet on medium high heat and add the remaining 1/2 cup of water. Stir in the 4 cups of sliced maitake mushrooms, 1/2 cup of chopped onion, and the 1/2 cup of chopped celery. Cook and stir for 5 minutes. Pour the 1 1/2 cup of chicken broth into a bowl and mix in the 2 tablespoons of corn starch, 2 tablespoons of soy sauce, tablespoons of parsley flakes, dried basil, teaspoon of ground oregano, 1/2 teaspoons of ground sage, marjoram, and rosemary. Pour into the cooked mushrooms and bring mixture to a boil on medium high. Add the 1 1/2 pounds of ground chicken and the rice. Stir and cook, it will thicken as it cooks. This dish is cooked when the chicken is no longer pink.

# Side Dish Recipes for Blood Type AB

## Basmati Rice

Sometimes a meal needs a good side dish of flavorful rice and this recipe fits the bill.

Makes 4 servings.

***Ingredients:***

*2 cups of chicken broth
*1 1/2 cup of basmati rice (uncooked)
*1/2 cup of water
*1/4 cup of onion
*4 tablespoons of butter
*1 teaspoon of salt
*1/2 teaspoon of turmeric
*1/2 teaspoon of garlic (minced)
*1/2 teaspoon of lemon juice.

***Directions:***

Add the 4 tablespoons of butter to a saucepan and heat on medium to melt the butter. Add the 1/4 cup of onions and sauté. Stir in the 1/2 teaspoon of minced garlic. Add the rice and stir for another 2 minutes. Pour in the 1/2 cup of water, teaspoon of salt, and the 1/2 teaspoon of turmeric and turn the heat to high. Stir constantly until the mixture comes to a boil, and then reduce heat to low and simmer, covered for another 20 minutes. Turn heat off and let it sit for 5 minutes. Place in a serving dish and sprinkle with the 1/2 teaspoon of lemon juice, fluff to mix and serve.

## Risotto Tomato Rice

This is a delicious Italian side dish rich in basil and it is absolutely tasty.

Makes 4 small servings or 2 large.

***Ingredients:***

*4 Roma tomatoes (peeled, seeded and diced)
*3 3/4 cups of tomato juice
*1 cup of Arborio rice
*1/2 cup of mozzarella cheese (grated)
*1/2 cup of basil (fresh chopped)
*1/4 cup of onion (chopped)
*1/4 cup of white wine
*3 tablespoons of butter
*2 teaspoons of garlic (minced)
*2 teaspoons of olive oil
*1/2 teaspoon of salt

***Directions:***

Add the 2 teaspoons of olive oil to a saucepan and turn to medium heat. Stir in the 1/4 cup of onions and sauté. Add the 2 teaspoons of minced garlic, stir, and cook for another minute. Stir in the cup of Arborio rice and stir for 2 minutes. Pour in the 1/4 cup of white wine and 3/4 cup of the tomato juice. Cook and stir until the rice absorbs all the liquid. Turn the heat to low and add the remainder of the 3 cups of tomato juice and stirring occasionally; cook until the rice is tender enough to eat. Turn the heat to medium, add the diced roma tomatoes, 1/3 cup of shredded mozzarella cheese, and stir until the cheese melts completely. Turn the heat off and stir in the 1/2 cup of fresh chopped basil and the 1/2 teaspoon of salt. Serve while hot.

# Conclusion

Please feel free to modify the recipes within this book, as cooking is like art, it changes with the user. Each recipe, though slated for one particular blood type, may be crossed over as good fits for the other blood types. The best thing to do is to memorize the allowable foods and avoidable foods for your particular blood type and make your own judgments on the recipes. Always seek the advice of your own health care provider before starting any new diet routine. Make sure you are getting all the nutrients your body needs in your diet.

# Section 2: Grain Free Recipes

There's something absolutely delicious about a freshly baked loaf of bread, a crispy waffle, or a tasty cake hot out of the oven! These foods all have one thing in common: they're made with grain or wheat flour. Cooking with wheat flour and grain is something that everyone does, and it produces a whole lot of delicious foods.

Unfortunately for many, grain and wheat are things that they cannot enjoy. Gluten intolerance can be a serious problem for many people, and they are unable to eat foods that contain lots of grain or wheat. When they do, they have serious digestive problems, or their body can react strongly and negatively to the gluten in the grain that they are eating.

Gluten has been linked to a number of problems. Interestingly enough, the body often sees gluten as being a foreign substance that it can't process. While gluten is commonly found in the food we eat, it wasn't always part of our diet. The human body can't always process this gooey, sticky protein easily, and it can be a bit hard on the body if you happen to be sensitive to it. Even those without celiac problems may not be able to handle the gluten, as their bodies react to the "foreign substance" by attacking it with antibodies.

Cutting grain out of your diet can help to reduce your risk of health problems, especially if you have celiac disorder or other gluten-sensitive problems. However, even for those that don't have these health problems, it may be a good idea to cut gluten out of your diet. Many people don't have celiac disease, and yet they still experience the drawbacks of eating gluten.

In an article in the New Zealand edition of Stuff magazine, an article by a world-renowned expert on food allergies, Dr. Rodney Ford, states, "Gluten causes tiredness, anxiety and stress. The medical world accepts it can damage the gut, but it can also damage the brain, skin and nerves. Until now, many of these illnesses have been blamed on everything from stress at home to other medical conditions, including
depression." [1]

Cutting gluten out of your life isn't just something you can do to prevent celiac problems, but it can be good for your health. Many holistic doctors and therapists will recommend cutting it from your diet, as it carries the risk of causing negative side effects.

Did you know that eliminating grain and gluten can be beneficial to your body? The benefits include:

- Reduced risk of IBS or other digestive problems
- Less chance of becoming fatigued, depressed, nauseous, or developing stomach cramps
- Boost in your energy levels
- Reduced body fat percentage
- Increase in lean muscle tissue
- Lowered blood pressure
- Improved mood and sense of wellbeing
- As you can see, there are many great reasons to cut grain from your diet!

"But," you may say, "all of my favorite foods are made with grain! How can I cut grain out of my diet and still enjoy the food I'm eating?"

Don't worry about it! In this book, you'll find plenty of delicious recipes that you can make without needing to use grain, and you can whip up your favorite dishes and still make them gluten-free. You'll have to spend a bit of money to stock your house with some ingredients you probably don't have right now, but you'll be amazed at how many delicious foods you can make without using grain.

Enjoy the book, and happy grain-free cooking!

# Tasty Grain Free Recipes

## Grain Free Breaded Chicken

There's nothing like some breaded chicken to kick off your lunch in style, but bread crumbs have wheat, right? Here is a quick and easy recipe you can use to make breaded chicken without the bread...

### Ingredients

For this dish, you will need:

1 large chicken breast
1 cup of almond flour
½ cup of Kraft's Parmesan Cheese
Thyme
Basil
Oregano
½ cup of butter
Red or crushed chili pepper
Garlic powder
Salt and pepper, to taste

**Preparation:**

To begin, slice the chicken breast into steaks -- preferably about three steaks from each half of the breast. You should have about 6 medium steaks from the breast.

Preheat your oven to about 350 F. Use a bit of butter to grease the bottom of a baking tray.

In a bowl, combine the almond flour with the Parmesan cheese. Sprinkle in about a teaspoon each of basil, thyme, and oregano, and add in a pinch of crushed red pepper for some spice. A teaspoon of garlic powder will help to add the flavor you want, and a bit of salt and black pepper will round out the flavors.

In a saucepan, melt the butter. Dip the chicken steaks into the butter, ensuring that the entire surface of the chicken is coated well. Roll the buttered strips in the almond flour, and make sure that they are properly coated with the flour mixture.

Place the steaks onto your baking tray, laying them as flat as possible. Transfer the tray into the oven, and let the steaks cook for about 20 minutes. They should be a wonderful golden brown, and they will be absolutely delightful to eat! (Check to make sure that they aren't pink in the center, as that's a sign that the chicken is undercooked.)

## Sesame Seed Chicken Fried Steak

Want to eat that Southern-style chicken fried steak that your mama used to make you? This simple recipe won't make it exactly like the regular steak, but it's as close as you'll get while on a gluten-free diet!

### Ingredients

For this dish, you will need:
4 large steaks, sliced fairly thin
2 eggs
½ cup of almond flour
1/3 cup of sesame seeds
1/4 cup of flax seeds
Chicken bouillon powder
Basil
Bay leaves
Garlic powder
Salt and black pepper, to taste

### Preparation:

To begin, place a pan on the stove to heat, and add in enough oil to deep fry your breaded steak. Let the oil heat as you go about preparing the rest of the meal.

Crack the 2 eggs into a bowl, and beat them vigorously to combine the egg and yolk. Add a pinch of salt into the eggs.

Combine the almond flour, a pinch each of chicken bouillon, garlic powder, salt, and pepper, and the flax seeds in a bowl. Add the sesame seeds into the bowl, and crush three bay leaves in your hands to add them into the mix. Use a fork to stir the dry ingredients together, and make sure that they're properly combined before moving on.

Dip each steak into the eggs, and roll the dipped meat into the flour and seed mixture. Make sure that the entire surface of the meat has been properly coated. If you want to really get the flour coating on right, you can roll the meat in the flour before dipping it into the egg, and roll it a second time after dipping to ensure that the layer of flour is very thick.

Place the steaks in the hot oil one at a time, and cook them until they are golden brown. Remove them from the pan once they are properly cooked, and place them on a plate with paper towels beneath and above them to soak up the oil.

Let the steaks sit until they are all cooked, transfer onto

a plate, and serve.

## Gluten and Sugar-Free Gingerbread Cake

Want a delicious dessert to make your Christmas celebrations complete? This gluten and sugar-free gingerbread cake will have all of the flavor of the holiday, but with none of the unhealthy nutrients that you're trying to avoid!

**Ingredients:**

For this cake, you will need:
½ cup of coconut flour
1 cup of amaranth flour
1 cup of buckwheat flour
2 tablespoons of flax meal (For those who want the non-vegan version of this cake, use 2 eggs instead of the flax meal. It will make the cake a bit fluffier, and will help to round out the flavors nicely.)
2 ½ teaspoons of baking soda
Ground cinnamon
Ground ginger
Ground cloves
Ground nutmeg
Salt
Water
¾ cup of agave nectar
¾ cup of molasses

Canola oil
Fresh ginger
Lemon zest

**Preparation:**

To begin, turn on the oven and let it heat to 350 F. As the oven is heating, prepare the cake.

Combine the coconut flour, amaranth flour, buckwheat flour, and baking soda in a bowl. Add in 2 teaspoons of cinnamon, the same amount of ground ginger, half a teaspoon each of cloves, salt, and nutmeg, and a teaspoon or two of lemon zest. Stir the ingredients well to combine.

In a separate bowl, combine the flax meal with a few tablespoons of water, and stir in the agave, the molasses, ¾ of a cup of canola oil, and a couple of teaspoons of the grated fresh ginger. Mix these ingredients together well, and pour them into the bowl with the dry ingredients. Stir the wet and dry ingredients together to make the batter for the cake, and add about a cup of boiling water to your final batter.

Once the water has been properly mixed in with the rest of the ingredients, pour the cake batter into a buttered baking pan. Place the pan into the oven, and let it cook for about 40 minutes.

You'll find that a toothpick or knife inserted into the center of the cake will come out clean, and it will let you know that your cake is ready to enjoy.

Cut once the cake has cooled a bit, and serve.

## Gluten Free Waffles

There's nothing like a heaping stack of waffles to get your morning started the right way, but your regular waffles are loaded with grain and gluten. These delicious grain-free waffles will be the perfect breakfast, and it will help you to enjoy what you're eating without having to worry about adding grain to your diet.

### Ingredients

For this dish, you will need:
1 cup of rice flour
1/3 cups of potato starch (not all cornstarch products are gluten-free)
3 tablespoons of tapioca flour
1 ½ teaspoons of baking powder
½ teaspoon of baking soda
Salt
Xanthan gum
Buttermilk
Sugar substitute
2 eggs
Canola oil
2 cups of water

### Preparation:

To begin, heat your waffle iron. It takes about 5 to 10 minutes for the waffle iron to heat -- depending on the brand -- so make sure that it's heating as you go about preparing the waffles.

Mix the rice flour, potato starch, tapioca flour, baking soda, and baking powder together in a bowl. Add in about half a teaspoon of salt, and the same amount of xanthan gum. Mix the dry ingredients together, and be sure that they are properly combined before moving on to the next step.

Crack the two eggs into another bowl, and add in the water. Add about 3 tablespoons of the oil, and mix the ingredients together well. Stir them in with the dry ingredients, and mix until you get the waffle batter you want. The batter will be a bit thick, so add buttermilk to produce the desired consistency for the waffle batter. Make sure that there are no lumps.

Use some spray cooking oil to grease the waffle iron, or use regular oil on a paper towel to cover the iron with a thin layer of oil. Pour the batter into the heated iron, and close the lid. Watch the waffle iron until the light turns off, and use a fork to remove the cooked waffle from the waffle maker.

Serve while hot, and enjoy the delicious, crunchy waffles!

## Buckwheat Pancakes

For those of you who just can't stay away from those flapjacks, this pancake recipe will be the perfect grain-free solution for you! You'll still be able to have a tall stack of delicious pancakes, but without worrying about gluten or grain.

### Ingredients

For this dish, you will need:
1 ½ cups of buckwheat flour
3 tablespoons of sugar (use sugar alternative for a low-sugar meal)
Salt
1 teaspoon of baking soda
Unsalted butter
1 egg
Buttermilk

### Preparation:

To begin, place a frying pan on the stove to heat. Make sure that it has been properly heated before placing the batter onto the pan, so give it time to warm up as you make the pancakes.

Mix the flour, sugar, and baking soda together in a bowl. Add in about a teaspoon of salt. Stir the ingredients well to combine.

Crack your egg in another bowl, and beat to combine the yolk and white.

Melt the butter in a saucepan or the microwave, and pour the melted butter over the flour mixture -- stirring as you pour. Add the egg into the mix, and pour in about a cup of buttermilk as well. Stir the batter together, and you'll have a fairly thick mixture. Keep pouring in buttermilk until your pancakes have reached the desired consistency, and stir to ensure that there are no lumps.

Once the batter has been prepared, pour it into a pitcher or an empty ketchup bottle. Gently pour or squeeze the batter onto your heated pan, which you will have coated with a bit of oil to butter to prevent the pancakes from sticking.

Cook until the top of the pancake is riddled with bubbles, and flip it over to cook on the other side for about 20 seconds.

Once the batter has been used up, you'll have a delicious stack of healthy buckwheat pancakes that are grain-free and fairly low calorie!

## Grain-Free Cornbread

You can't have chili beans without some delicious cornbread, and there are so many other dishes that won't be complete without this delicious savory baked bread. Don't worry about it being high in grain, as we've substituted the ingredients in the bread for grain-free ones!

### Ingredients

For this dish, you will need:
1 ½ cups of cornmeal
1 cup of millet flour
1 cup of rice flour
2 eggs
Water
Vegetable oil
¼ cup of sugar
1 tablespoon of baking powder
Salt

### Preparation:

To begin, heat your oven to about 400 degrees. This way, it will be hot enough to cook the bread, but it won't be so hot that the bread will burn.

Use a bit of butter to grease a 9x9 baking dish, and set it aside as you prepare the bread.

In a bowl, crack and beat the eggs vigorously to combine the yolk and egg white. Heat 1 ½ cups of water until they are lukewarm, and add them into the eggs. Drop in ¼ cup of canola or vegetable oil, and mix the ingredients well until they are properly blended.

In a separate bowl, mix the millet flour, rice flour, and cornmeal together. Add in the white sugar, the baking powder, and about a teaspoon of salt. Make sure that the dry ingredients are all mixed together properly, and hollow out a hole in the center of the bowl.

Pour the wet ingredients into the hollowed center of the flour mixture, and use a whisk to stir the ingredients together properly. Whisk and stir until you are sure that there are no lumps, which could take a few minutes.

Once you're sure there are no lumps, pour the batter into the greased baking pan. Place the pan into the oven, and let it cook for about 20 minutes. You can tell that it's cooked by pressing on the surface of the bread. If it's properly done, the corn bread will spring back up when you press gently on it.

Remove from the oven, let the cornbread cool for a few minutes, and serve while still warm.

## Curried Quinoa

This delicious side dish is made without any grain, which means that you can eat it whenever you want! The quinoa is a much lower-calorie alternative to rice, but it will be a delicious alternative that will make the dish absolutely fantastic!

**Ingredients:**

For this dish, you will need:
1 cup of quinoa
Olive oil
1 onion
Garlic
2 cups of chicken broth
Curry powder
Ancho chili powder
Salt and pepper

Preparation:

To begin, place a skillet on the stove to heat. Bring it to medium heat, and pour a couple of tablespoons of olive oil into the pan.

Chop the onion very finely, and add between 3 and 5

cloves of garlic -- depending on your flavor preference. Cook the aromatics in the oil, leaving them in the pan for about 5 minutes to ensure that you have extracted the flavor from them. Add the quinoa into the pan, and cook the seed in the oil until it is lightly toasted.

Once you're done cooking the quinoa, pour the chicken broth into the pan. Cover the pan, and let the broth heat until it begins to boil. Stir in about a tablespoon each of the curry powder and Mexican chili powder, and cover the pan once again.

Turn the heat down to let the quinoa simmer, and let it cook on low heat for about 25 minutes. The quinoa should be soft and tasty, and you can add a bit of salt and pepper to add the flavor you want for the dish. (Serve as the starch with nearly any protein, and it will be a delicious companion for your meal!)

## Roasted Almond Cookies

Want to enjoy a delicious dessert without getting into the grain-loaded cookie jar? These cookies are quick and easy to make, and you'll find that they're the perfect grain-free solution to help you stay true to your gluten-free diet!

**Ingredients:**

For this dish, you will need:
1 cup of raw almonds
½ cup of maple syrup
1 cup of oat flour
Almond extract

**Preparation:**

Preheat the oven to about 275 F, which will be hot enough to toast the almonds.

Place the cup of almonds onto a baking sheet, and put them in the oven. Let them heat until they become golden brown and are releasing a delightful scent, which will take about 40 minutes. Be careful that they don't burn.

Once the almonds are cooked, remove them from the oven and set them aside to cool. After they have cooled down enough, run them through your food processor to produce a fine almond flour.

Mix the flour in a bowl together with the oat flour, maple syrup, and almond extract.

Turn the heat of the oven up to 350 F, and let it heat.

As the oven is heating, use your hands to form the dough into 6 balls. Press the balls gently to flatten them a bit, until they are about half an inch thick. Place the cookies onto a greased baking sheet, and put the sheet in the oven.

Let the cookies bake for about 12 minutes, but keep a close eye on them because the edges can burn very quickly. They will become browned and crisp around the edges of the cookie, and that's how you'll know that they're done.

Remove them from the oven, let them cool, and enjoy!

## Grain-Free Zucchini Bread

Most people think of banana bread or carrot cake as being the only vegetable-laden desserts that you can make, but you'll find that zucchini bread will be a delicious alternative that will be just as healthy and tasty! Thanks to the grain-free recipe, you won't have to worry about the gluten.

**Ingredients:**

For this dish, you will need:
1 cup of teff flour
1 cup of buckwheat flour
Baking soda
Salt
Baking powder
3 eggs
Lemon zest
Cinnamon
1 cup of apple sauce
½ cup of maple syrup
Coconut oil
Vanilla extract
2 cups of grated zucchini
1 cup of raisins and almonds mixed

**Preparation:**

To begin, turn on your oven and pre-heat it to about 350 degrees. As it's heating, move on to the next step.

Mix the buckwheat and teff flours together in a bowl, and add in a tablespoon of cinnamon, a teaspoon of salt and lemon zest each, 2 teaspoons of the baking soda, and ¼ teaspoon of baking powder. Stir well to ensure that the ingredients are properly combined before moving on.

In a separate bowl, combine the apple sauce and maple syrup together, and crack the three eggs into the bowl. Beat well to mix the ingredients, and add two teaspoons of vanilla extract and a tablespoon of coconut oil into the bowl. Stir well to mix.

Once the wet ingredients are properly mixed, pour the dry ingredients into the bowl. Stir well or use an electric mixer to combine the ingredients, and stir until there are no more lumps. Pour the zucchini into the batter, and add the raisins and almonds as well. Mix to distribute these ingredients.

Pour the batter into a greased baking pan, which should have a bit of butter along the bottom to help make the cake tasty. Put the pan into the oven, and let it cook for about 50 minutes. The cake will take longer to cook than your average flour cake, but you'll know that it's done when a toothpick or knife inserted into the center of the cake comes out clean.

Remove the cake from the oven, let cool for a few minutes, cut, and serve!

## Apple Cobbler

Not quite the same as Apple Crumble, this Apple Cobbler recipe is the perfect grain-free breakfast treat! It will be crunchy, flavorful, and delightful, but it won't have any of the gluten that you're trying so hard to avoid.

### Ingredients

For this dish, you will need:
6 apples
1 can of cranberry sauce
Brown sugar
1 cup of steel-cut oats
Cinnamon
Soy milk
Butter

Preparation:

To begin, peel and cut the apples. You will want to make them small slices, easy enough to fit into your mouth without being too small.

Preheat the oven to about 350 F once the apples are done. Grease a baking tray with a bit of butter, and set it aside as you move on.

Combine the apples and the cranberry sauce in a bowl, and add in 2 or 3 tablespoons of the brown sugar. Add ¼ cup of soy milk, and mix the ingredients well to ensure that they are properly combined.

Melt a bit of butter on the stove, and pour the butter over the top of the oats. Toss the oats to coat them evenly with the butter.

Place the apple mixture into the pan, and cover it with a top layer of oats. Place the pan into the oven, and let it cook for about 35 or 40 minutes. You'll see that the oats turn a pleasant golden brown, and the juices released by the apple and cranberry sauce will bubble nicely.

Remove from the oven, let cool for a few minutes, and serve as the perfect healthy breakfast!

## Breakfast Cereal Sans Gluten

A healthy breakfast cereal can be the perfect thing to get your morning started the right way, as it will provide you with slow-burning carbs that will give you energy all day long. This breakfast cereal will be perfect, as it comes without grain and will give you that energy boost you need for the long day ahead.

**Ingredients:**

For this dish, you will need:
½ cup of quinoa
½ cup of buckwheat groats
1 cup of brown basmati rice
½ cup of millet
½ cup of flax seeds
½ cup of sesame seeds
½ cup of cornmeal
½ cup of amaranth

**Preparation:**

To begin, place the basmati rice into a blender or grinder, and grind until you have produced a coarse rice flour. Empty the rice into a bowl.

Grind or blend all of the other ingredients, and you will end up with a mixture of various flours -- none of which will be wheat or grain flour, of course.

To prepare the cereal, put 4 cups of water into a pan to boil on the stove. Once the water is boiling, add in about a cup of the cereal mixture and a pinch of salt. Add a tablespoon or two of milk powder, and let the ingredients cook until they have thickened.

To add some flavor, add in a bit of cinnamon, some butter, and a tablespoon of sugar. You'll find that these ingredients will sweeten the cereal, and a bit of milk will help to make it more edible.

The cereal mixture will take about 20 minutes to cook, and you should keep the heat low to prevent it from burning. After 20 minutes has passed, scoop into a bowl, let cool for a minute, and enjoy!

## Rice Stuffing

Need to stuff that Thanksgiving turkey but don't want to use bread? This rice turkey or chicken stuffing will be the perfect thing for you! It's tasty, subtle, and easy to make, and it will enable you to give your turkey the right filling.

### Ingredients:

For this dish, you will need:
2 cups of white rice
Water
Chicken bouillon
1 onion
Butter
Garlic
1 celery stalk
Parsley
Salt
Sage
Thyme
Pepper, to taste

### Preparation:

To begin, you will need to dice the onions as fine as you

can. Make sure to chop the onions very small.

Place a pot on the stove to heat, and add about a tablespoon of butter into the bottom of the pan. Once the butter has melted, add the onions into the mixture. Let the onions fry for a minute, and chop the garlic as you do so. Add about 5 cloves of garlic -- chopped fine -- into the pan, and fry the garlic along with the onions.

Once the onions have begun to brown around the edges, add the uncooked rice into the pan. You will want to cook the rice until it shows signs of beginning to burn, and the grains will become slightly browned. At this point, add the 2 cups of water into the pan, and cover it.

Once the rice begins to simmer, add a tablespoon or two of chicken bouillon into the pan. Dice the celery stalk, and drop the pieces into the pan. Sprinkle parsley, salt, sage, thyme, and all the pepper you want into the rice.

The simmering water will cook the rice in about 20 minutes, but keep a close eye on it. once the level of the rice rises above the water level, you only have about 5 to 7 more minutes until the rice is completely cooked. Make sure the rice doesn't burn, and don't let it cook all the way. The rice should still be a bit crunchy when you turn it off.

Once the rice is cooked, remove it from the pan, let it cool, and use it to stuff your turkey. The partially cooked rice will finish cooking as the turkey cooks, and it will come out soft and fluffy!

## Gluten Free Irish Shortbread

There's nothing like a good piece of Irish shortbread to eat after your Irish beef stew, and you'll find that a hearty piece of this bread will go down nicely. The best part about this bread: it's made without gluten or wheat!

### Ingredients

For this dish, you will need:
2 cups of butter
2 cups of rye flour
1 cup of corn flour
2 cups of brown sugar

### Preparation:

To begin, heat the oven to 300 degrees. Take the time to grease two baking pans, or use grease paper to prevent a mess.

Soften the butter in a double boiler, or leave it at room temperature for an hour to make it easier to mash. Use a fork to mix the sugar into the butter, and combine it until it is creamy and blended. Add the corn flour and the rye flour, and combine into a nice dough.

Divide the dough that you have into two portions, and press each portion of dough into the pans that you have prepared. Use the fork to prick some shallow holes, dividing the bread into individual portions. You can sprinkle a bit of sugar to make it decorative.

Place the baking pans into the oven, and let them cook for about an hour. You'll find that the bread can cook in as little time as 45 minutes, so keep an eye on it. You may notice that the edges of the bread are getting browned, and the top will be nicely golden.

Cut the bread into individual pieces while it is still warm, and enjoy!

## Asian Sesame Noodles

If you love the taste of the Orient, this will definitely be the dish for you. These tasty noodles are grain-free, but they're absolutely delightful! With the right ingredients added to this dish, you'll have everything you need to get your Oriental on!

**Ingredients**

For this dish, you will need:
400 grams of Gluten-free noodles
Sesame oil
2 carrots
Garlic
Fresh ginger root
1 onion
½ head of cabbage
½ pepper
1 sprig of cilantro
Almond butter
Gluten-free soy sauce

**Preparation:**

To begin, you'll need to put a pot of water on the stove to boil. Add about 3 cups of water per 100 grams of noodles, and give it a few minutes to boil.

As the water is heating up, dice the ginger, garlic, and onions. You can use as much garlic as you want, but add no more than a teaspoon of fresh ginger root. Julienne the carrots, the bell pepper, and the cabbage, making the slices as thin as possible.

Place a wok on the stove to heat, and pour in a few tablespoons of sesame oil. Once the oil is hot, drop in the ginger, garlic, and onions. Stir fry the ingredients for a few minutes, and add in the carrots. Once the carrots have begun to soften, add in the peppers and the cabbage. Cook for just 3 minutes, and add the soy sauce into the mixture.

Place the noodles in the water to cook, and keep a close eye on them. You don't want them to overcook, as they'll be quite unpleasant. Make sure that they're al dente, and remove them from the stove. Drain the water, run cold water over the noodles, and throw the noodles into the wok.

Stir fry the noodles with the other ingredients, adding a tablespoon of almond butter, 2 tablespoons of soy sauce, and ½ tablespoon of sesame oil to flavor the noodles. Cook until the liquid has all been eliminated from the wok, leaving you with a dry, slightly fried noodle dish.

Serve the noodles onto two plates, chop the cilantro to sprinkle on top of the noodles, and serve with chopsticks and your favorite Chinese hot sauce.

## Shrimp Cakes

Want to enjoy some seafood, but can't eat gluten? These gluten-free shrimp cakes are an absolute delight, and they'll help you to get a lot more protein in your diet. They're fairly easy to make, but they're definitely a delicious meal that will be ideal for anyone on a weight loss diet.

### Ingredients

For this dish, you will need:
1 pound of shrimp
1 red bell pepper
2 cloves of garlic
Scallions
Lime juice
Sea salt
Chipotle
1 egg
½ cup of almond flour
Grapeseed or peanut
½ cup of chopped cilantro

### Preparation:

To begin, peel and de-vein the shrimp. This can be a

lengthy process, so be prepared to spend at least 20 minutes in this activity.

Once the shrimp has been prepared, throw them into the blender or food processor. Press the pulse button until the shrimp has been chopped fine, and remove the shrimp from the blender.

Pour the shrimp into a bowl, and add a teaspoon of sea salt, the cilantro, and ¼ teaspoon of chipotle. Crack the egg into the bowl, and mix it well to combine.

Dice the scallions, the garlic, and the bell pepper, making sure that they are very finely chopped. Add them into the bowl, and stir to mix properly. Add the lime juice for the finishing flavor touches.

Use your hands to form the ingredients into balls, which you will dip into the almond flour to coat them thoroughly as you flatten them into patties.

Place a skillet on the stove to heat, and add enough oil to fry the patties. Place four of the patties into the skillet at a time, and cook for about 5 minutes. Turn the patty onto its other side, and cook it until that side is also browned.

Remove the cooked patties from the pan, and place them on a paper towel to drain as you cook the rest. You should obtain about 12 patties from this mixture.

Enjoy with a simple marinara sauce, or just pour some of your favorite hot sauce over the patties to make them taste delicious!

## Stuffed Bell Peppers

This dish is made with a rice stuffing that will be absolutely divine, not to mention free of gluten. If you want to enjoy a delicious stuffed bell pepper, this is a recipe that you must try!

**Ingredients:**

For this dish, you will need:
6 green bell peppers
Diced green chilies
1 pound of ground beef
1 onion
5 cloves of garlic
1 cup of rice
Cumin
Cilantro
Chili powder
Sea salt

**Preparation:**

To begin, place a pan on the stove to heat. Pour a tablespoon of oil into the bottom of the pan, and dice one of the cloves of garlic. Cook the garlic until it's nicely browned, and add the rice into the pan. Once the rice is toasted, pour 1 cup of water into the pan. Cover it and cook on low heat until the rice is done. Remove from the heat and set aside.

Dice the onion and the rest of the garlic very finely, and place a skillet on the stove to heat. With a bit of oil in the bottom of the pan, sauté the garlic and onions for a few minutes. Add the ground beef into the pan, and cook it until it's well done. Add ½ can of diced green chilies 3 minutes before the meat is done, and cook them with the meat. Once you have turned off the meat, add in a teaspoon of cumin, ½ cup of diced fresh cilantro, a teaspoon of chili powder, and a tablespoon of sea salt.

Take the ground beef mixture and add it into the pan with the rice. Mix well to combine, and add salt and pepper as desired.

Use a knife to score around the top of the bell pepper, and pull off the top to extract the seeds. Wash the peppers thoroughly to remove any remaining seeds.

Heat the oven to 350 F.

Use a spoon to scoop the rice and beef mixture into the bell peppers, stuffing them completely full. Remove the seeds from the tops of the bell peppers, and place the tops back on the peppers. Place the bell peppers on a tray, and place the tray in the oven.

Let the peppers cook for about 45 minutes to an hour, and they will be ready to eat!

## Gluten-Free Turkey Club

This is a delicious sandwich that you can make all on your own, and you'll be able to use gluten-free bread to slap together this quick and easy meal. You can used gluten-free bread that you bought from the store, or you can make your own loaf of gluten-free nut bread. This recipe will just tell you how to make the perfect sandwich, but there's a recipe further down that will tell you how to make the bread.

**Ingredients**

For this dish, you will need:
3 slices of gluten-free bread
4 slices of turkey ham
1 avocado
2 slices of your favorite cheese
Onion
Tomato
Canned chipotle chili peppers
Lettuce
Pickles
Alfalfa sprouts
Dijon mustard
Tabasco sauce
Light mayonnaise

**Preparation:**

To begin, place a skillet on the stove to heat. Once the skillet is properly hot, place the bread on the skillet. Only toast one side of two slices of bread, but toast the third slice on both sides.

Remove the bread from the skillet, and start with one of the half-toasted slices placed toasted side down.

Onto this slice of bread, spread a bit of mayonnaise. Add 2 slices of turkey, one slice of cheese, 1 onion ring, two pickles, and the alfalfa sprouts. Sprinkle Tabasco sauce generously. Grab the fully toasted slice of bread, and spread Dijon mustard on one side and mayo on the other. Place the toast mustard side down on top of the other ingredients.

Add the last two slices of turkey onto the sandwich, along with the cheese, 1 slice of tomato, 1 diced canned chipotle pepper, 3 slices of avocado, and two leaves of lettuce. Sprinkle Tabasco sauce generously onto the sandwich, and spread Dijon mustard onto the untoasted side of the final piece of bread before completing your sandwich.

Cut in half, serve, and enjoy!

## All Purpose, Gluten and Grain-Free Nut Bread

This is the nut bread that you can use to make sandwiches, cheese toast, eat with your morning coffee, or just snack on when you're hungry. It's a gluten and grain-free bread that you can use for just about anything, and it will be the perfect option regardless of what sweet or savory dish you need bread for. It's also quick and easy to make!

**Ingredients:**

For this dish, you will need:
¼ cup of flax meal
1 ½ cups of almond flour
Salt
4 eggs
½ teaspoon of baking soda
1 cup of walnuts, hazelnuts, almonds, and other nuts.
¼ cup of sesame seeds
¼ cup of amaranth
¼ cup of sunflower seeds
1 teaspoon of apple cider vinegar
1 teaspoon of agave honey

**Preparation:**

To begin, heat the oven to about 350 F, and grease two bread pans.

Combine the almond flour with the flax meal, baking soda, and a pinch of salt in a bowl, stirring well to ensure that the ingredients are properly combined.

Crack the eggs into a bowl, and use a fork or whisk to beat them well. Make sure they are frothy, and add into the bowl the agave honey and vinegar. Mix the wet and dry ingredients together in a bowl, and add the various nuts and seeds into the same bowl. Use a fork or whisk to mix the ingredients properly until there are no lumps.

Pour the bread batter into the greased bread pans, and put them in the oven. The bread will probably take about 30 to 40 minutes to cook, so keep an eye on them. Check the bread for doneness by inserting a knife into the center, and it will come out clean when it's done cooking.

Remove from the oven, set aside to cool, and slice the bread once it has reached room temperature. You now have the ideal loaf of bread for just about anything!

## Pad Thai

Pad Thai is one of the most popular Thai dishes in the country, and it will be a wonderful grain-free alternative to the more popular Chinese and Japanese fried noodle dishes. It's fairly easy to make, and it's absolutely delicious!

### Ingredients

For this dish, you will need:
6 ounces of rice noodles
Sesame oil
1 onion
1 head of broccoli
Water
4 cloves of garlic
Scallions
Cilantro
Peanuts
Salt and pepper, to taste

### Preparation:

To begin, place a pot of water on the stove to boil. Bring the water to a boil, and drop the rice noodles in to cook. The package will usually have clear instructions on how to cook the noodles, so follow them precisely for al dente noodles. Drain the noodles, run cold water over them, and set them aside.

Place a skillet on the stove to heat, and add a bit of sesame oil into the bottom. Dice the onion very fine, and add it into the pan to be sautéed. Cook the onions on medium-low heat, and make sure they are nicely browned.

As the onions are cooking, cut the broccoli into bite-sized spears. Once about 10 minutes has passed, add the broccoli in with the browned onions. Add ¼ cup of water, and cover the pan. Let the broccoli sauté with the onions for roughly 5 minutes, after which time it will become soft and turn a bright color.

Add salt to the pan, and dice the garlic to be added as well. Add a bit more sesame oil to ensure that the ingredients don't dry out, and add some diced peanuts into the pan. Use a tablespoon of arrowroot powder and water to thicken the mixture, and stir fry the ingredients to ensure that the powder is spread all around.

Place the noodles onto a plate, and pour the vegetable mixture over the top. If you want to add some protein, throw some shrimp into a pan and grill them to serve on top of the vegetables and noodles.

Garnish with some scallions and diced cilantro, and enjoy!

## Gluten-Free Chicken Noodle Soup

There's nothing like a cup of chicken noodle soup when you're feeling ill, but wheat noodles would just make the problem worse. With this grain-free chicken noodle soup, you'll always feel better, and it is a tasty soup that you can't help but love!

**Ingredients:**

For this dish, you will need:
1 liter of chicken broth
1 stalk of celery
1 onions
3 cloves of garlic
1 carrot
1 zucchini
1 pack of gluten-free noodles
½ chicken breast

**Preparation:**

To begin, dice the onions and the carrots very finely. Make sure that they are diced very small.

Place a pot on the stove to heat, and drop a tablespoon of olive oil into the bottom. Add the garlic and onions into the pot, and sauté them until they are browned.

Once the onions and garlic are properly cooked, add the chicken broth into the pot. Set the heat on medium, and let the broth boil.

As the broth is heating up, cut the carrots into small pieces about as large as your fingernails. Throw them into the pot, along with the celery - which you will slice into small pieces as well.

Run the zucchini through a julienne slicer, and you'll have what looks like simple noodles. Put them into the pot, and let them cook along with the other ingredients.

On the side, add a bit of butter into a skillet. Slice the chicken breast into small chunks, and cook the chicken in the pot until browned on the outside. Add the partially cooked chicken into the pot of soup, ensuring that you get all the liquid and oil from the skillet.

Turn the soup up to high heat, and let it cook for another 15 minutes. Once that time has passed, drop the gluten-free soup noodles into the mixture, and let them cook on low heat. Once the noodles have cooked properly, turn off the fire and remove the pot from the stove.

Serve, add a splash of lime, and enjoy!

## Gluten-Free Potato Beef Stew

Want to make a thick, hearty stew without adding flour or wheat to the mixture? This delicious stew will be an ideal meal to have on a cold winter evening, and it will be just as rich and hearty as any stew made with flour to thicken it!

Ingredients:

For this dish, you will need:
4 potatoes
1 pound of stew meat
2 carrots
1 onion
5 cloves of garlic
½ cup of table wine
¼ cup of soy sauce
1 cup of milk
2 liters of beef broth
Salt and pepper, to taste
Preparations:

To begin, peel one potato, dice it, and place it in a small pot of water to boil. Let the potato cook for about an hour, adding more water into the pot whenever necessary. Once the potato has cooked for the prescribed 60 minutes, drain all but the final dregs of water, mash with a fork, and set aside.

Place a soup pot on the stove to heat, along with a couple of tablespoons of peanut oil in the bottom of the pot.

Dice the onion and the garlic, and add them into the pot to sauté. Add the onions first, and let them cook until nearly browned before adding in the garlic.

Dice the stew meat into small bite-sized pieces, and add them into the pot once the garlic has been properly cooked. Cook the meat until it has been browned on the outside, and add the beef broth into the pot. Bring the beef broth to a boil as you cut the other vegetables.

Cut the potatoes into medium-sized cubes, and add them into the pot. Peel and cut the potatoes into slices, and add them into the pot.

Let the stew boil for about 20 minutes, or until you're sure the potatoes are nearly cooked. Add in the soy sauce, table wine, and the milk, and let it keep cooking. Add salt and pepper as desired, along with crushed bay leaves for added flavor.

Just 5 minutes before you are about to turn the soup off, add in the mashed potato. Stir the soup well, ensuring that the mashed potato is diluted properly. The starch from the potato will thicken the stew, but it will ensure that the other ingredients aren't overcooked.

Serve with nut bread, and enjoy!

## Grain-Free Ideal Breakfast

The ideal way to start the day is with a rich breakfast, but the average breakfast consists of grain-laden toast, pancakes, or other things that are made with grain. If you want the perfect breakfast without adding grain to your diet, this is the recipe for you!

**Ingredients:**

For this dish, you will need:
3 eggs
2 slices of turkey or Canadian bacon
6 oranges
2 Slices of Nut bread (see recipe above)
Butter
Honey
Coffee

**Preparation:**

To begin, place a skillet on the stove to heat. Once the skillet is hot, add the bacon and cook until done. Remove the bacon from the stove, and place on a paper towel to drain.

Leaving the bacon grease in the bottom of the pan, let it

reheat until ready for the eggs. Crack one egg into the pan, and crack the other two eggs into a cup -- making sure to get only the egg whites. Add the two egg whites into the pan, and cook the eggs until done as desired. (If you don't like your eggs to be liquid on the top, flip them over and let them sit in the pan for 3 seconds before scooping them onto your plate.)
Add the slices of nut bread onto the plate, along with the Canadian or turkey bacon. Spread butter and honey as desired on the bread, and serve yourself a cup of coffee.

Squeeze the oranges, and enjoy your fresh cup of OJ for the ideal grain-free breakfast!

## Dark Chicken Soup

If you're not too particular about the way your soup looks, you'll find that this will be the ideal meal for you! It comes loaded with all the nutrients you need, and there are even a few noodles floating around to help fill you up. All in all, however, it's a nicely low calorie meal - and grain-free as well!

**Ingredients**

For this dish, you will need:
2 liters of chicken broth
1 bunch of chard
2 carrots
1 bunch of spinach
1 cup of shitake mushrooms
1 pack of shitake mushroom noodles
¼ pound of chicken breast

**Preparation:**

To begin, place the chard and spinach in a pot with 2 cups of water and 2 cups of chicken stock. Bring the veggies to a boil, and let them cook until they are soft. Pour the soup into the food processor, blend it until it is completely liquefied, and set it aside.

Pour the chicken broth into a pot, and bring it to a boil. Cut the carrots and shitake mushrooms into slices, and add them into the soup. Pour the liquefied dark greens into the pot, and let them cook along with the chicken broth.

In a pan on the side, add a pat of butter into the bottom as the pan heats. Dice the chicken breast into chunks, and let the breast cook until it is browned on the outside. Once it is nearly cooked, pour the chicken and the grease into the soup pot. Let it cook until you're sure the chicken is thoroughly done.

Add the mushroom noodles a few minutes before you want to cook the soup, and follow the cooking instructions on the package. The noodles shouldn't take too long to cook, and you can serve out the soup while it's still piping hot!

## Carrot Muffins

These delicious muffins will help you to start the day out right, and you can munch on a couple of them as you head to work. Thanks to the fact that they're completely grain-free, they'll be the perfect option for you!

### Ingredients

For this dish, you will need:
¼ teaspoon of baking soda
¼ cup of coconut flour
Cinnamon
3 eggs
Salt
¼ cup of oil
¼ cup of natural molasses
Vanilla
3 carrots
¼ cup of raspberries, blackberries, and black currants

### Preparation:

To begin, preheat the oven to about 350 F. This is the perfect temperature for muffins, as it will keep cooking time down without risking burning the muffins.

Combine the baking soda, coconut flour, and a teaspoon of cinnamon in a bowl, and stir it well to ensure that it's properly combined.

In a separate bowl, crack and mix the eggs. Whip them until they are frothy, and pour the oil, molasses, and a teaspoon of vanilla into the mix. Beat well, add a pinch of salt, and combine the wet ingredients with the dry.

Use a whisk to combine the wet and dry ingredients well, and stir until you are sure there are no lumps.

With a bit of butter, grease a muffin tray. You'll get about 12 to 18 medium-sized muffins, though as many as 30 mini muffins. Put the tray into the oven, and cook the muffins for about 30 minutes. Insert a knife into the top of one muffin, and it should come out clean once it's done.

Remove the muffins from the oven, scoop them out of their tray, and set them aside to cool.

## Almond and Grilled Chicken Salad

The beauty of salads is that they are some of the best grain-free recipes, and you won't have to worry about getting gluten if you eat a healthy salad. If you want to really go all out with the salad, add nuts and lots of filling veggies! You'll find that it will be tasty and very enjoyable!

**Ingredients:**

For this dish, you will need:
1 pound of chicken breast
1 head of Romaine or Iceberg lettuce
1 cup of raw almonds
1 cup of raw peanuts
1 cup of dried cranberries
1 apple
½ cup of olive oil
½ cup of apple cider vinegar
1 cup of gluten-free soy sauce
Salt
Sesame seeds

**Preparation:**

To begin, slice the chicken breast into steaks about ¾

inch thick. You'll get about 3 steaks from a single chicken breast. Place the chicken breast on a grill, and rub a seasoning of salt, pepper, garlic, and Parmesan cheese onto the breast before cooking it. Grill the chicken well on both sides, and make sure that the middle of the chicken is cooked before removing it from the grill. Set the chicken aside.

Soak the lettuce in a bowl of ice cold water, which will make it crunchy and crispy. Once the lettuce has soaked for 30 minutes, use your hands to rip it into bite-sized leaves.

Slice the apple into quarters, cut out the cores, and cut the apple into small chunks. Add the apples into the salad, along with the cranberries.

In a skillet on the stove, place the almonds and peanuts together. The raw nuts will need to be toasted, and they will take about 20 minutes. Make sure to stir them every 5 minutes or so, and keep the heat on medium high to prevent them from burning. Once the almonds and peanuts are toasted, add them into the salad.

Slice the chicken breast into strips, and add them into the salad as well.

Combine the vinegar, soy sauce, and olive oil together, along with a pinch of salt and some black pepper. Pour this mixture over the salad, and sprinkle sesame seeds liberally on top to garnish the salad. It's now ready for you to eat!

## Gluten-Free Breakfast Biscuits

There's nothing like a delicious, buttery biscuit to start your day off on the right foot, and these grain-free biscuits will be just what you need to enjoy your morning. They're easy to whip up, and you can take them with you to snack in your car on the way to work.

**Ingredients**

For this dish, you will need:
2 cups of almond flour
½ teaspoon of baking soda
2 eggs
1 teaspoon of honey
1/3 cup of butter or margarine
Salt

**Preparation:**

To begin, preheat the oven to about 350 F. This is the temperature that will allow the biscuits to turn golden brown on the outside, but without making the center of the biscuits too dry.

In a bowl, combine the almond flour with the baking soda and a pinch of salt. Stir well to ensure that there are no clumps of baking soda.

In another bowl, crack the eggs and beat them until they are frothy. Add in the butter and the honey, and beat well. You'll want to keep stirring until you have a slightly creamy mixture.

Fold the wet ingredients gently into the dry ones, and mix until you're sure that there are no lumps. You will need to keep stirring as the dough is formed.

Use a piece of greased baking paper to roll the biscuit dough out, and keep rolling until you've flattened the dough to about 1 ½ inches thick. Use a jar with a wide mouth to cut out the biscuits, and keep rolling the dough until you have turned it all into biscuits.

Transfer the biscuits to an oven tray with a piece of greased baking paper, and put the tray into the oven. Let the biscuits cook for about 15 minutes, and keep a close eye on them. You'll notice that the rounded edges of the biscuits will start to brown, and don't let them get too dark before removing them from the oven.

Use a spatula to scrape the biscuits off the greased baking sheet, and set them on a rack to cool. Once they're cool, spread a bit of butter and honey on them, and enjoy!

## Nutty Granola

Granola is one of the best breakfasts that you can have, and you'll find that this nutty granola will be just the thing to stoke up your internal furnace first thing in the morning. It's a grain-free breakfast that will kick off your day in style!

### Ingredients

For this dish, you will need:
1 cup of steel cut oats
2 cups of almonds
1 cup of amaranth
1 cup of raisins
1 cup of walnuts
1 tablespoon of vanilla
Butter
Cinnamon
Sugar

### Preparation:

To begin, place a skillet on the stove to heat. Melt a cup of butter in the bottom of the skillet, and add the oats in once the butter is liquefied completely.

Use a spatula or wooden spoon to roll the oats thoroughly in the butter, and ensure that the oats are properly coated. Remove the skillet from the heat, and transfer the oats into a flat baking tray.

Preheat the oven to 350 F.

Add the raisins into the oats, and cut the almonds and walnuts in half. Add in the amaranth, and sprinkle a bit of sugar, cinnamon, and a few tablespoons of vanilla extract onto the oats. Make sure that the oats are mixed properly, and put the tray into the oven to cook.

Give the oats about 30 minutes to cook at 350 F, but keep checking them to ensure that they don't burn. You'll find that they'll become nice and crunchy once they've cooked properly, but let them cool down before eating them.

## Grain-Free Breakfast Bars

Need something quick to munch on as you drive to work in the morning? Don't let the heavy traffic get you down, but make these delicious breakfast bars to help keep your mind off the fact that you're sitting and doing nothing. They're a healthy breakfast that you can enjoy on the go!

**Ingredients**

For this dish, you will need:
2 cups of almond flour
1/3 teaspoon of baking soda
1/3 cup of grapeseed oil
Vanilla extract
1/3 cup of honey
½ cup of shredded coconut
1/3 cup of raisins
1/3 cup of nuts (your preference)
¼ cup of flax seeds
¼ cup of amaranth
¼ pumpkin seeds

**Preparation:**

To begin, preheat the oven to 350 F.

In a bowl, combine the almond flour with a pinch of salt and the baking soda. Make sure to mix well, as that will eliminate any lumps of baking soda.

In another bowl, mix the honey with a tablespoon of vanilla and the grapeseed oil. The oil will be a bit hard to mix in, but a bit of effort will yield a properly mixed liquid.

Pour the wet ingredients in with the dry ones, and whisk vigorously to ensure that the wet and dry ingredients combine nicely without any lumps.

Once you're done mixing, add the nuts, seeds, raisins, coconut, and amaranth into the batter. Mix well to distribute the latest additions.

Use a bit of butter to grease the bottom of a baking tray, and pour the mixture into the pan. Place the pan in the oven, and let it cook for about 20 minutes at 350 F. You'll find that it turns a nice golden brown, and it will become very crunchy and a bit hard to cut.

Slice the bars into small pieces, and serve or set aside to eat on the go.

## Garden-Style Hot Dogs

Hot dogs are one of the most popular American foods around, but the problem is the hot dog bun. If you want to enjoy a classic hot dog in a very unique way, these garden-style hot dogs will be an ideal way for you to eliminate the gluten from your meal.

**Ingredients:**

For this dish, you will need:
6 hot dogs
6 slices of bacon
1 head of Romaine lettuce
½ tomato
½ onion
Pickle relish
Sauerkraut
Ketchup
Mayo
Mustard
Tabasco sauce

**Preparation:**

To begin, soak the head of lettuce in ice cold water. The cold water will help to make the lettuce crunchier and crispier, which will make it much easier to eat.

Place a skillet on the stove, and let it heat. As the pan is heating, wrap one strip of bacon around each hotdog. You can hold the bacon in place using toothpicks, but make sure that the toothpicks don't interfere with the cooking process.

Let the hot dogs cook for about 20 minutes on low heat, and turn them regularly to ensure that they don't burn. The grease from the bacon will make them very tasty.

Once they're thoroughly cooked, remove the skillet from the stove, but leave the hot dogs inside.

Remove 12 strips of lettuce, and make 6 stacks of two leaves. Dice the tomato and the onions, making sure that they are very small.

Place a bit of sauerkraut in **the bottom** layer of lettuce, and stack the second leaf on top. Place each hot dog into the top leaf, and add tomato, onion, and pickle relish on top. Add the condiments of your choice, and enjoy the delicious, all-natural hot dog meal!

## Grain-Free Mac and Cheese

Mac and Cheese is the quintessential American meal, but egg noodles are made with wheat. Using gluten-free noodles will allow you to still enjoy this delicious dish, but without having to worry about adding grain to your meal!

### Ingredients

For this dish, you will need:
2 packs of gluten-free noodles
3 cups of grated cheddar cheese
½ cup of butter
1 ½ cups of milk
2 tablespoons of heavy cream
¼ pound of bacon
1 onion
4 cloves of garlic

### Preparation:

To begin, place a skillet on the stove to heat. Add a bit of butter into the bottom of the skillet, and dice the onions as the pan gets hot. Add the onions into the bottom of the pan to sauté, and dice the garlic to add in once the onions begin to brown.

Remove the garlic and onions from the stove once the aroma of the garlic is extracted, and slice the bacon as the skillet heats up once again. Place a pot of water on the stove to boil, which will be for the noodles.

Once the skillet is hot, add the bacon into the pan. Cook until it is nicely browned, and remove from the stove.

Place the onions and garlic back on the stove, and pour the milk and bacon into the pan. Once the milk gets hot, add in the heavy cream and the butter. Bring the ingredients to a boil, and add the cheddar cheese into the mix. Turn the fire off, but leave the pan on the stove.

Boil the noodles, and cook them until they are al dente. Place the noodles back into the pot they were cooked in, add the cheese sauce over the top, garnish with a bit more cheese, and serve while hot!

## Almond Raisin Muffins

These muffins are simple and easy to make, but they'll be delicious without a doubt! You can even top them with icing to make delicious cupcakes, or keep them light if you're on a diet! Enjoy them no matter where you are, as they are fantastic.

**Ingredients:**

For this dish, you will need:
1 cup of flax meal
1 cup of almond flour
1 tablespoon of baking powder
Nutmeg
Cinnamon
½ cup of raisins
1/3 cup of toasted **almonds**
1 stick of butter
Salt
4 eggs
½ cup of sugar
½ cup of buttermilk
2 tablespoons of brown sugar

**Preparation:**

To begin, you will need to heat the oven to about 375 F. Once the oven is hot, turn it down to 350 F, which is the ideal temperature for baking the muffins.

Combine the baking powder, flax meal, almond flour, and a pinch of salt in a bowl, mixing well to combine. Add a teaspoon each of cinnamon and nutmeg, and stir well.

Combine the butter, eggs, sugar, and milk in a bowl, and beat until the eggs are frothy and the butter is creamy. Using melted butter will make the process a lot quicker, but you can use an egg beater if you don't want to take the time to melt the butter.

Combine the wet and dry ingredients, and mix them well to eliminate any lumps. Add the raisins into the mix. Chop the toasted almonds into small pieces, and add them into the muffin batter as well.

Once the ingredients are all stirred in well, pour the muffin batter into a muffin baking tray. Use paper muffin cups if you want to limit the mess.

Place the muffins in the oven, and let them cook for roughly 15 to 20 minutes, depending the altitude of your city(it takes longer for things to bake the higher above sea level you are). Insert a toothpick into the top of the muffins when they look cooked, and they are done when the toothpick comes out clean.

Remove the muffins from the tray, set them aside to cool, and serve.

## Grain-Free Pizza

Pizza is one of the most popular dishes in the world, but it's hard to make a good pizza without using flour. This pizza is made without wheat, and it's a tasty alternative that gluten-sensitive people can enjoy without worrying about their stomachs acting up.

### Ingredients

For this dish, you will need:

1 cup of quinoa flour
1 cup of potato flour
1 cup of almond flour
1 cup of buckwheat
Salt
Xanthan gum
4 teaspoons of dried yeast
Canola or olive oil
Water
Tomato sauce
Cheese
Pizza toppings of your choice

### Preparation:

To begin, heat the oven to a toasty 350 F.

Grease some baking sheets with a bit of olive or canola oil, and place them on the trays where you will be cooking your pizza.

Sift the various flours, salt, and baking soda into a bowl, and combine the dry ingredients well. Add the yeast into the mixture.

Mix half a liter of warm water with a couple of tablespoons of olive oil, and add the wet ingredients into the dry ones. Mix the dough until it is properly combined, and set it aside for a few minutes to rise.

Once it has risen, use a spoon to scoop it into your pizza tray. Make a nicely rounded pizza, and put it in the oven to cook until the crust is golden brown.

All that is left to do is to scoop the pizza or tomato sauce onto the top of the crust, add cheese, and top with the ingredients of your choice. Put the crust back into the oven, and cook it until the cheese has properly melted.

Slice, serve, and enjoy!

# Your Grain Free Meal Plan

So, you've got all these awesome grain-free recipes to work with! Whether you're trying to lose weight or just stay healthy, eating these foods will help you to keep grain and gluten out of your life. If you want to add these delicious meals to your diet, here is an 11-day meal plan that you can use to incorporate all of these recipes into your life:

**Day 1:**
Breakfast: Buckwheat Pancakes
Lunch: Eggs and Nut Bread Toast
Dinner: Pad Thai

**Day 2:**
Breakfast: Gluten Free Waffles
Lunch: Grain-Free Cornbread with Grilled Chicken or Steak, plus plenty of veggies
Dinner: Special K cereal (made with rice rather than wheat flour)

**Day 3:**
Breakfast: Special K Cereal
Lunch: Stuffed Bell Peppers
Dinner: Chicken with Rice Stuffing

Dessert: Roasted Almond Cookies

**Day 4:**
Breakfast: Apple Cobbler
Lunch: Asian Sesame Noodles
Dinner: Almond and Grilled Chicken Salad

**Day 5:**
Breakfast: Breakfast Cereal Sans Gluten
Lunch: Grain Free Breaded Chicken with Nut Bread and veggies
Dinner: Gluten-Free Chicken Noodle Soup with Nut Bread
Dessert: Gluten and Sugar-Free Gingerbread Cake

**Day 6:**
Breakfast: Carrot Muffins
Lunch: Gluten-Free Turkey Club
Dinner: Curried Quinoa with Chick Peas

**Day 7:**
Breakfast: Grain-Free Ideal Breakfast
Lunch: Dark Chicken Soup with Nut Bread
Dinner: Grain-Free Mac and Cheese

**Day 8:**
Breakfast: Gluten-Free Breakfast Biscuits

Lunch: Gluten-Free Potato Beef Stew
Dinner: Shrimp Cakes
Dessert: Gluten-Free Irish Shortbread

**Day 9:**
Breakfast: Nutty Granola
Lunch: Dark Chicken Soup with Nut Bread
Dinner: Special K Cereal

**Day 10:**
Breakfast: Breakfast Bars
Lunch: Garden-Style Hot Dogs
Dinner: Sesame Seed Chicken Fried Steak

**Day 11:**
Breakfast: Almond Flour Muffins
Lunch: Grain-Free Pizza
Dinner: Special K Cereal

The meal plan above doesn't come with the calorie count on each food item, but that's something that won't be as important as the fact that they are all grain-free foods. You can eat them without worrying too much about calories, but try and keep the consumption of these foods to a healthy minimum in order to avoid gaining weight!

All of these recipes can be found online, though some of them are our own original creations. You can probably find similar recipes on websites like AllRecpes.com, About.com, and particularly ElanasPantry.com. They are all recipes that someone made, and we just wanted to share them with you. We've made a few adjustments to the various recipes so that you'll get only our unique grain-free flavor on the recipes, but you'll find that there are many like them. The important thing is that you can enjoy your grain-free cooking and eating, and we wanted to provide you with a recipe book that you can use to prepare delicious meals free of grain and gluten. We apologize if you've seen these recipes elsewhere, and we hope that you enjoy the creations we have presented to you!

**[1]** http://www.stuff.co.nz/life-style/38883/The-effects-of-gluten-on-health

www.ingramcontent.com/pod-product-compliance
Ingram Content Group UK Ltd.
Pitfield, Milton Keynes, MK11 3LW, UK
UKHW020142250726
13967UKWH00002B/823